At the King's Table

Where the Broken Are Beloved

LISA WILT

Abingdon Women
Your Life. Your Faith.

At the King's Table

Where the Broken Are Beloved

ISBN 978-1-7910-4352-0

Cover description: Watercolor artwork depicts a place setting with a white dinner plate centered on the cover, surrounded by soft floral accents and gold flatware. The title, *At the King's Table*, appears in decorative purple and gold lettering, with the subtitle *Where the Broken Are Beloved* in an arc beneath the plate. Additional text identifies the book as *A Study in 2 Samuel*, lists the author as Lisa Wilt, and notes that video access and a leader guide are included.

MANUFACTURED IN THE UNITED STATES OF AMERICA

This book is dedicated to anyone who has ever felt ...

broken,

alone,

lost,

hurt,

fearful,

shamed,

forgotten,

or orphaned.

Our King of kings invites you

to sit with Him and His family

every day for the rest of your life.

At the King's Table: Where the Broken Are Beloved.

Don't wait for heaven to take your seat!

WATCH YOUR STUDY ANYTIME, ANYWHERE.

Access your *At the King's Table* videos on any device with your Amplify Media account.

GET STARTED IN TWO STEPS

1 **Scan the QR code** or go to **My.AmplifyMedia.com/amplify/redeem**

2 **Create your free account** and enter your companion code

Companion Code
LW34T8GG

KEEP TRACK OF YOUR LOG IN INFO

Email ____________________

Password ____________________

Companion code subject to expiration. Code may be redeemed only by the recipient of this book. Code may not be transferred or sold separately. Internet connection required.

ONCE YOU'RE IN

- Your videos are saved to your account
- Watch anytime on phone, tablet, or TV
- Come back anytime at My.AmplifyMedia.com

AMPLIFY™ MEDIA

Contents

About the Author

Hi, I'm Lisa. I'm a small-town gal with God-sized dreams. I'm a retired pharmacist who once dispensed meds but now dispenses encouragement by pairing beloved Scriptures with fresh stories through women's Bible studies, devotionals, speaking, a daily radio ministry, and my podcast, *1-Minute WOW Words*. While I'm a Bible teacher, my favorite titles are Gigi to Elijah and Gideon; proud mama to Alyssa and Garrett and forever wife to David.

Ministry has always been a passion of mine. Throughout my years as a pharmacist, I also wrote and taught Sunday school curriculum, directed the women's ministry in my home church, and chaired the hospitality team. These days, I get to do what I love most—write Bible resources for women. Because let's face it: Life can be hard, and we all need encouragement (me included!). When the world feels heavy, God's promises are like spiritual confetti—bright, beautiful, and ready to lift our hearts.

Life's responsibilities and frustrations can make us weary, which is why we need Jesus. Daily, we will experience speed bumps that slow us down, but if we keep our eyes on Jesus, they can't stop us from reaching the finish line—where we will stand before God's throne and hear "Well done, good and faithful servant."

Let's have fun while we run this race together,

Lisa

Facebook	@LisaWiltMinistries
Instagram	@lisa_wilt_author
YouTube Channel	@lisa_wilt_author
Website	LisaWilt.com

About This Study

In this six-week study, you and your group will explore the tender and transformative story of Mephibosheth, a forgotten prince (son of Jonathan and grandson of King Saul) who is carried from hiding to honor when he is given a seat at King David's table. His story reminds us that even though we are broken and blemished, we are invited to come to our King's table, where we find complete and perfect love.

We'll begin our journey with some brief backstory found in 1 Samuel, setting the stage for Mephibosheth's story. Then we'll dive into the twenty verses in 2 Samuel that form the heart of this study. For the first four weeks, we'll move through these verses line by line. As we do, I'll share rich connections to the stories of other biblical characters. You'll have space to trace how Mephibosheth's story links to the larger story of our King revealed throughout the Scriptures—and to your own story as well.

In week 5, we'll step back to view Mephibosheth within the broader context of David's story in the second half of 2 Samuel. These chapters are marked by battles and betrayals, yet Mephibosheth stands out as one who guards his heart, staying faithful to the king. Here we'll explore how he models trustworthiness and contentment in the midst of turmoil and conniving, ultimately experiencing peace when David returns to the throne.

In our final week together, we'll widen our focus even further. Looking across all of Scripture, we'll consider how Mephibosheth's story affirms God's continuous story of steadfast love woven through both the Old and New Testaments.

Mephibosheth has a hard name to pronounce and hard breaks to endure. Maybe you've had hard breaks too. Maybe you need mercy and grace. Don't we all? When I look at **Me**phibosheth, I see **me**... and you... and anyone who has ever felt less than, rejected, or lonely. If you've ever been wounded by rejection or loneliness, you'll find in his story a King who is faithful, forgiving, and—best of all—trustworthy.

Throughout our journey, we'll turn to the King of kings to provide hope in each day's Scriptures, stories, and reflective questions. Our goal is to discover a loving God who seeks us out, calls us by name, lifts us from our lowest places, and covers our wounds with grace. He longs to heal our hurts, remove our shame, and calm our fears.

Like Mephibosheth, we don't need to hide because the King wants to restore our inheritance and trade our shame for robes of righteousness. In this life, we will experience battles and betrayals, hardships and heartbreaks, but at the heart of this study is a simple and life-changing truth: Even in the places where we feel broken, we are cherished, chosen, and invited to sit with the King of kings!

What to Expect

This six-week study offers five daily lessons each week. As I was writing the lessons, I pictured you sitting with Jesus and me. I didn't picture Jesus scowling at us—not once. And I didn't picture Him as somber either. Jesus was an engaging storyteller, so you'll find stories tucked into every lesson because we remember and relate to stories.

Life can be hard enough without having a hard Bible study. So here's my promise:

- I will tell stories that move your heart, stretch your mind, and draw you closer to the King of kings.
- I will be creative so that learning feels light, not heavy.

Each week includes a memory verse. At the end of the first day's lesson, you'll review the full verse. On the second day, one word of the verse will be left blank for you to fill in. And on each day that follows, an additional word will be left blank. This gradual approach to memorization will help the verse settle gently and naturally into your mind and heart.

You'll also find a QR code that you can use to link to a worship song related to the day's theme, helping you to pause, breathe, and rest in God's presence—along with a blessing written in first-person, present tense as if Jesus is speaking directly to you, bringing comfort and healing. Prayer is simply a conversation with God, so let these words that reflect the heart of Jesus open that conversation within you.

A bonus feature is a weekly recipe chosen to echo the week's theme, so that when you gather in sweet fellowship, you can "taste and see that the Lord is good" (Psalm 34:8a). Consider it an invitation not only to know about God's goodness but also to experience it personally. My hope is that someone will volunteer to prepare the recipe each week and bring it to your group meeting to share.

Because we are called to serve, I encourage everyone to bring an item each week for the food pantry so that others can know, in a tangible way, that God loves them and desires to provide for their table. Check with your church or local food pantry for suggested items.

It is my hope that as you move through each week, God gently reshapes the way you see yourself. May His love cover every broken place so completely that you wake each day knowing that, even with your flaws, you are deeply beloved.

God delights in you. He invites you to come to Him when you're hungry for affirmation, when you need strength for the day, and when you long for hope to lift you out of despair. When you come to His table, let your soul be filled to overflowing. Taste His kindness, feel His love, and trust that He truly delights in you.

His desire is for you to take your rightful seat at His table, where the broken are beloved. Don't wait for heaven to accept His invitation. His table is set for you today.

Sending you lasting joy,

Lisa

Week 1

Feeling Broken

Memory Verse

But he was hurt because of us; he suffered so.
Our wrongdoing wounded and *crushed him.*
He endured the breaking that made us whole.
The injuries he suffered became our healing.

—Isaiah 53:5 *The Voice (emphasis added)*

Recipe of the Week

Simple and scrumptious, these Oreo cookie balls are a favorite recipe. I've renamed them *Trinity Truffles* because they're made with three main ingredients and reflect three qualities of a great recipe: fancy enough to feel special, fast enough to make with little ones, and easy enough to share with joy. They're a sweet reminder that God delights in using the simple and ordinary to create something extraordinary.

Introduction to This Week

2 Samuel 4:4

Welcome, friends! This week we meet Mephibosheth in 2 Samuel 4:4. At just five years old, his world was forever changed by trauma. His granddad, King Saul, and his father, Prince Jonathan, were killed in battle. In the panic that followed, his nanny fled with him—but in the chaos, she dropped him. That fall left his body broken, and the loss of his family left his spirit wounded.

How does a child begin to carry such pain? For Mephibosheth, his broken body gave way to broken thinking and a broken spirit. Isn't that often our story too? We face moments when life shatters. Our bodies ache, our minds spiral, and our spirits grow weary. Relationships fracture, and the world feels heavy. Like Mephibosheth, we are tempted to retreat, convinced our brokenness defines us. This week we will explore some of the ways we experience brokenness and how they can remind us of our need for healing from One greater than ourselves.

Day 1: Broken Body

Biblical Foundations:
1 Samuel 18:1-4; 20:14-17; 23:16-18; 2 Samuel 4:4a

Focus Scripture:
(Saul's son Jonathan had a son named Mephibosheth, who was crippled as a child.)
—2 Samuel 4:4a

Today we begin our journey with Mephibosheth, whose broken body gave way to broken thinking and a broken spirit. Since I take my cues from Jesus, the greatest storyteller in the history of the world, I want to start with a story about my daughter who broke baby Jesus one Christmas. Almost two years old and barely tall enough to stretch her pudgy little hand up into the Nativity manger, she kidnapped the ceramic figure.

He was just the right size. She knew she was only supposed to look at the baby and not touch, yet it was doubly thrilling to have Jesus in her hands. As any wannabe momma, Alyssa wanted to rock her baby. So she tugged her tiny rocking chair from her carpeted bedroom into the tiled kitchen.

It was a special chair with a music box on the bottom curved band that played lullabies when fueled by movement. She was smart and knew that the chair had to be on a hard surface for the music box to work.

Before she sat down, she needed a blanket to swaddle her baby. A dishcloth would do, and she knew just where to find one. She felt so *big!* Everything was perfect until the unthinkable happened.

Alyssa dropped baby Jesus. His body broke in half. She cried. I cried.

Why couldn't she have broken a leg off a sheep or a tail off a cow? She loved the animals too. But baby Jesus? He was the *pièce de résistance.* This was our most exquisite Christmas decoration—handmade by an older couple in our church.

Every year it was the first decoration to be set up and the last to be taken down—displayed in the highest place of honor, right inside our front door for everyone to see. I treasured it. But as I looked into Alyssa's teary eyes, I knew she was sorry. She wanted me to make it better.

Unlike Humpty-Dumpty, it didn't take all the king's horses and all the king's men, just me and Mr. Elmer, to put baby Jesus back together again.

Remembering this story of our baby Jesus being dropped and broken reminds me of the biblical story of another child being dropped and broken. His name was Mephibosheth. We'll call him Sheth for short.

Once upon a time, Sheth was born into royalty. His father was a brave prince and first in line to ascend to the throne. His grandfather was the first king of Israel, and wow, did he look the part. If there ever was a better model of tall, dark, and handsome, Israel hadn't laid eyes on him. Saul was head and shoulders taller than anyone else in the land. And don't you know that the fair ladies of the kingdom must have fallen head over heels for him. After all, he was God's answer to the people's prayer.

Like the surrounding nations, Israel wanted a king—one they could see and touch. So God gave them a *looker*. Saul *looked* very good. But here's the thing. Saul struggled with pride. He was haughty and thought he could make his own rules with an **EGO** that ultimately **E**dged **G**od **O**ut. He rewrote the rules, disobeyed God, and acted impulsively time after time. God's Spirit left Saul. Later Saul consulted a medium. He is the only king in Israel's history who actively sought a medium for guidance.

Sadly, Saul's desire for power consumed his thoughts, stole his peace, and drove him to madness. In bitter rage, he even turned against his own son, Jonathan, because he had befriended David. The Bible tells us that Jonathan and David shared a rare friendship.

Read 1 Samuel 18:1-4, the first covenant promise between Jonathan and David, and summarize the passage in your own words below:

Have you ever experienced ***an immediate bond*** like this when someone was willing to lift you up at their own personal expense? If so, describe it below:

What four things did Jonathan give to David?

Jonathan loved David "as his own soul" (1 Samuel 18:3 ESV) and gave him his tunic, sword, bow, and belt. These are royal symbols that foreshadow David's future kingship, not Jonathan's.

The friendship between David and Jonathan shines as one of Scripture's brightest portraits of *phileo* love, which is loyal affection—a bond rooted in shared courage, mutual honor, and deep trust.

Read 1 Samuel 20:14-17, the second covenant promise. If Jonathan were to die, what did he ask of David?

Jonathan asked David to treat his family with the faithful love they shared. This covenantal love forms the backstory for our six-week study.

The Old Testament word for the flawless way God loves us is embodied in the Hebrew word *hesed*, which appears nearly 250 times. Sometimes we see it spelled with a silent *c* as *chesed.*

This Hebrew word is translated in many ways—steadfast love, grace, mercy, loving-kindness, covenant faithfulness, loyalty, devotion, and goodness. These synonyms help expand our understanding, but they only skim the surface of this rich, multifaceted word. *Hesed* is love in action. In English, we don't have a single word that fully captures its essence or magnitude. We use the word *love* for everything from green beans to grandparents. Do you remember when you were in grade school and your teacher asked you to use a new word you had learned in a sentence to show you understood it? Isaiah does this for us.

Read Isaiah 54:10 in the margin and underline the English words used to describe God's *hesed* love.

"Though the mountains be
shaken
and the hills be removed,
yet my unfailing love for you
will not be shaken
nor my covenant of peace
be removed,"
says the LORD, who has
compassion on you.
—Isaiah 54:10 NIV

You may have underlined "unfailing love" *[hesed]* or the entire phrase "my unfailing love for you will not be shaken." That's a beautiful assurance.

To summarize, *phileo* speaks of the affectionate, brotherly love that binds people together in genuine friendship, and *hesed* describes God's covenant-faithful love—His steady, loyal mercy that acts on behalf of His people even when they falter. God's covenantal love is the overarching commitment He makes to His people, and *hesed* is the way He faithfully lives out that commitment of love throughout history. Together, these words reveal a God who loves with unwavering faithfulness, relational warmth, and deep delight in His people.

Now read 1 Samuel 23:16-18a, the third and final covenant promise between David and Jonathan. How did Jonathan encourage David, and what did he promise?

Their covenant is renewed in the wilderness while David is running from King Saul. Jonathan strengthens David and affirms David's future kingship rather than his own. These three moments trace the deepening of their bond—from friendship, to loyalty under threat, to spiritual solidarity in suffering.

David likely spent about seven to ten years living in caves and hiding from Saul.[1] Having been anointed king years earlier by Samuel, David finally assumes the throne and strengthens the nation, winning battle after battle against Israel's enemies.

Whew! We just covered more than a decade. Now that we know the backstory, we get to meet Mephibosheth as we jump forward into King David's reign.

Read 2 Samuel 4:4a in the margin. What are the punctuation marks that set off this verse?

(Saul's son Jonathan had a son named Mephibosheth, who was crippled as a child.)

—2 Samuel 4:4a

Mephibosheth was once royalty, and now he is sandwiched between parentheses as an afterthought. That's not exactly a regal entrance. It's more of an oh-by-the-way-I-forgot-to-mention-this-kid-with-a-disability mention. Once favored but now forlorn. Sheth doesn't even get his own chapter. (Just. One. Verse.)

Have you ever been introduced in a way that made you feel marginalized or insignificant? If so, describe it below.

Today our Focus Scripture is 2 Samuel 4:4a, which tells us that Mephibosheth was crippled as a child. Like Sheth, we all experience physical brokenness. Sometimes it shows up in the fleeting nuisance of a cold. Other times it comes in the crushing weight of injuries sustained in an accident, leaving us in chronic pain—something my husband has lived with for over thirty years. I have a two-inch-long scar on my neck from the removal of my thyroid to avoid a suspected malignant tumor from spreading. Many of us have known the anguish of cancer that leaves us weak.

Though we may not walk with a visible limp as Sheth did, we can stagger under the unseen and often unspoken burdens of illness and frailty. Fibromyalgia is one such invisible burden. Tinnitus, ringing in ears, is another. There are countless others.

What physical ailments—both acute and chronic, visible and invisible—do you carry?

What other physical ailments affect someone you love?

As a former pharmacist, I wish I had the magic pill that could cure all sickness. I don't. While we all will experience physical brokenness, it will be limited to earth. The excellent news is that Jesus was broken so we could be whole forever in heaven!

Reread this week's memory verse:

> *But he was hurt because of us;* he suffered so.
> *Our wrongdoing* wounded and *crushed him.*
> ***He endured the breaking that made us whole.***
> *The injuries he suffered became our healing.*
> —Isaiah 53:5 *The Voice (emphasis added)*

What stands out to you in this verse?

When would you have been willing to take on an illness so that someone else, perhaps a child, would not have had to bear that pain?

Let this prayer—written in first-person, present tense, as if Jesus is speaking directly to you—bring comfort and healing. Prayer is a conversation with God, so allow these words that reflect the heart of Jesus to begin the conversation. Write your name in the blank and let this become the blessing Jesus whispers over your heart.

Enter into a time of worship. Scan this QR code to listen to "Scars in Heaven" by Casting Crowns.

My beloved____________________, I see your pain and weariness. When your body feels fragile, lean into Me. I am not distant from your suffering. I walked roads of pain too. I know what it is to hurt, and I hold you with a tenderness that never lets go.

I am strengthening you in ways you cannot see. I am shaping hope in you that pain cannot steal. I am preparing a place where your body will be restored and your joy made complete. Until that day, rest in Me. Let My love remind you that you are never alone. You are held. And one day, you will be whole.

Now offer your response: *Jesus, . . .*

Day 2: Broken Relationships

Biblical Foundations:
2 Samuel 4:4b; John 4:1-42

Focus Scripture:
[Mephibosheth] was five years old when the report came from Jezreel that Saul and Jonathan had been killed in battle. —2 Samuel 4:4b

As women, we are wonderfully relational. God wired us so that engaging with others brings color, depth, and meaning to our lives. Because of this, we feel deeply when relationships shift, strain, or break.

Many of us can relate to the quiet ache of relational hurt. Some aches are small and pass quickly—like when an acquaintance makes a sharp comment that catches us off guard. It stings, but the sting fades.

Other wounds linger. A misunderstanding with a coworker or a friend can result in hurt feelings, distance, or words we wish could be taken back. These moments remind us how much connection matters and how tender our hearts really are.

Today, we pause to acknowledge those places—not alone, but in community. And we invite God to meet us gently in every ache.

Name a time when a broken relationship left you feeling hurt.

Put a check mark beside any responses that describe how you reacted.

_____ went silent

_____ lashed out with harsh words

_____ shared the experience with a close friend to seek comfort

_____ prayed about it

_____ went directly to the person in private to gain understanding

Sometimes the pain reaches even deeper, when a sibling or parent criticizes us, passes judgment, or expresses long-held disappointment. These fractures can grow, leaving families struggling to gather around the table. The hope is that healing will come and relationships will be restored before death robs us of the chance to mend what has been broken.

Reread today's Focus Scripture, 2 Samuel 4:4b (page 20). What was the report, and how old was Mephibosheth at the time?

Regardless of our age, we grieve the loss of those we love. Though Mephibosheth was only five when Jonathan died, he was old enough to remember his dad. Perhaps Sheth remembered the warm smile he could hear in his father's voice when he said, "I love you, son." Maybe he remembered a bedtime lullaby, sung softly in the dark. Sheth likely remembered any endearing nickname his dad called him. (We'll talk more about names in the weeks to come.) Maybe Jonathan hoisted young Sheth onto his shoulders the way my own dad once lifted me. Sheth might have wrapped his arms around his father's neck, hugging him tightly as they tromped through their royal home in Gibeah—that Benjaminite hill town perched just north of Jerusalem.

I recently lost my dad after his sixteen-year battle with Parkinson's disease and dementia. Even now, I can't imagine losing him when I was Sheth's tender age of five. Jesus knew the loss of His earthly father. Scripture implies that Joseph died before Jesus began His public ministry, which means Jesus stepped into His calling carrying the quiet ache of having lost the man who raised Him.

Jesus also knew the sting of broken relationships—rejected in His own synagogue (Luke 4:16-30) and later misunderstood by His own family (Mark 3:20-21) as He walked in obedience to His mission. It's comforting to know we have a Savior who understands both grief that lingers and relationships that wound.

Perhaps this is why the longest recorded conversation Jesus has with a single person in Scripture occurs when He speaks to the woman at the well—a woman who knew the pain of five broken relationships. Jesus met her with compassion, truth, and restoring grace, just as He meets us in our own places of loss and longing.

The forty-two verses of John 4 feel like they should come with a soundtrack—something hopeful, maybe with a little sparkle—because this is the moment Jesus breaks every social rule and rewrites the script for who gets to belong, be seen, and carry His message. It's a story that starts with tension, takes a surprising turn at Jacob's well near Sychar—a small Samaritan village—and ends with a whole town buzzing because one woman dared to run with good news.

To appreciate the shock factor of this encounter, it helps to know the backstory between Jews and Samaritans. Centuries earlier, when the Northern Kingdom of Israel was conquered, many Israelites intermarried with the surrounding nations. Their descendants became the Samaritans. Jews in the south, who prided themselves on maintaining ethnic and religious purity, saw Samaritans as half-breeds, heretics, and compromised people who worshipped in the wrong place with the wrong traditions.

Samaritans, for their part, weren't sending the Jews holiday cards either. The hostility was mutual, deep, and long-standing. So when Jesus, a Jewish rabbi, strolls into Samaria, He's already crossing a line. When He sits down at Jacob's well and strikes up a conversation with a Samaritan woman, He's basically blowing up the whole rulebook.

This woman comes to the well at noon, the hottest part of the day, when no one else would be there. Women normally drew water in groups early in the morning or late in the evening. The fact that she comes alone suggests she's avoiding people, maybe because people have been avoiding her. Her heart is likely heavier than the water jar she carries.

She's carrying not just a water jar but a lifetime of whispers, side-eyes, and social exclusion. A Jewish rabbi would never speak to a *Samaritan*, period. A Jewish man would never speak to a *woman* alone in public. And a rabbi would certainly never speak to a *woman with a complicated past*. She checks all three boxes on the "Do Not Engage" list. Yet Jesus chooses her.

When have you felt set aside, unseen, or quietly placed on the "Do Not Engage" list?

Turn to John 4 and hold your place there. Read verses 6-8 and step into the scene for a moment. What do you notice, feel, or hear? What do you imagine Jesus's tone of voice to be?

Jesus starts this historic conversation with a simple request: "Please give me a drink" (v. 7). It sounds ordinary, but it's revolutionary. He's asking to drink from her vessel, which would make Him ceremonially unclean according to Jewish tradition. She knows this, which is why she basically says, "Um . . . are you sure you're talking to the right person?" Jesus responds by offering her something far better than well water: *living water*.

In the ancient world, "living water" meant flowing water—fresh, moving, spring-fed water. But Jesus is talking about something deeper. He's offering her spiritual renewal, inner cleansing, and a relationship that satisfies the deepest places of longing. She's intrigued but still thinking in literal terms.

Read her response in John 4:11. Sketch below what she says Jesus is missing.

Then Jesus gently shifts the conversation from water to her life. He tells her to call her husband, and she admits she doesn't have one. Jesus affirms her honesty and reveals that He knows she has had five husbands and is now living with a man who isn't one. He doesn't shame her. (There's more to come on erasing shame next week.) He doesn't lecture her. He simply names her reality with compassion and clarity.

I believe this is because Jesus knows her pain. She may not have been a scandalous figure at all, but a wounded one. In her world, a husband could dismiss a wife for something as heartbreaking as infertility, leaving her with no voice and no protection. Seen through that lens, her five marriages could reflect the quiet sorrow of barrenness.

Whatever the cause of the severed relationships, Jesus speaks to her with dignity. It's the first moment she realizes this stranger sees her and doesn't turn away.

Have you ever experienced someone looking past your history and recognizing your worth as a person deeply seen? If so, describe that experience briefly. If not, reflect on what it might be like to be seen without judgment.

Now read John 4:25-30. What does Jesus tell her about Himself?

What do you imagine this dear woman felt in that moment?

This is the moment I want to cheer! It's the first time Jesus openly declares *He is the Messiah* to an adult in a public conversation. Not His disciples. Not the religious leaders. Not a king or a priest. A *woman* who has suffered broken relationships becomes the first person to hear Jesus say, "I am he" (John 4:26 NIV).

I laugh at what happens next because it's so like me. She leaves her water jar behind—just as I'm forever leaving my water bottle in random places—but she has a good reason. Once you've tasted living water, old containers don't matter anymore.

The woman who once avoided people becomes the first evangelist in history! She doesn't deliver a polished sermon or quote Scripture. She simply says, "Come see a man who told me everything I ever did" (John 4:39, author's paraphrase). Her testimony is honest and compelling—a reminder of what truly reaches people: our story of how Jesus met us in our broken moments. God doesn't require polish or perfection. He uses authenticity. She shares her story, and it works. The people listen and believe.

Meanwhile, the disciples return from their grocery run and are baffled to find Jesus talking to a woman. Jesus uses the moment to teach them that His mission is bigger than their categories. The harvest is ready, He says, and sometimes the people you least expect are the ones most ready to receive the good news.

When has God used an unexpected person to speak a humble, heartfelt blessing of the good news into your life?

How has God used the brokenness in your story to reach people?

The disciples are learning that the kingdom of God is not a gated community; it's a wide-open invitation. Many more believed—and it all started when a woman carrying the weight of broken relationships simply shared her story. Her life reminds us that God uses imperfect people like you and me. In fact, in His hands, our brokenness can become a bridge to reach others who have walked similar roads. With God, nothing is wasted—even things we deem broken and unusable.

Enter into a time of worship. Scan this QR code to listen to "Woman at the Well" by Olivia Lane.

Reread this week's memory verse and fill in the blank:

But he was __________ *because of us*; he suffered so.
Our wrongdoing wounded and *crushed him.*
He endured the breaking that made us whole.
The injuries he suffered became our healing.
—Isaiah 53:5 *The Voice (emphasis added)*

Write your name in the blank and let this become the blessing Jesus whispers over your heart.

My beloved_______________, I see the ache you carry from broken relationships. Mephibosheth lost his father as a child, and you have known loss too. I walked that road when Joseph died, and the woman at the well carried the weight of five shattered vows. None of this pain is hidden from Me. You may feel broken, but I want you to know that you are deeply loved. Come to Me with every wound and let My presence be your steady place, your living water, your true belonging.

Now offer your response: *Jesus, . . .*

Day 3: Broken Thinking

Biblical Foundations:
2 Samuel 4:4c; Philippians 4:8

Focus Scripture:
When the child's nurse heard the news, she picked him up and fled.
—2 Samuel 4:4c

Yesterday we explored the hurt from broken relationships in our own lives and in the life of the first evangelist: the woman at the well. This woman came to draw water at noon, choosing the hottest, loneliest hour of the day because she hoped to avoid the judgments of others.

Instead, she encountered the most important person she would ever meet: Jesus. Just like her, we can meet Jesus in the ordinary, unnoticed moments of our days, even as we answer emails, fold laundry, wash dishes, or run errands. These everyday spaces can become sacred spaces when Jesus steps into them.

Before meeting Jesus, I imagine this Samaritan woman, like so many of us, had internalized her imperfections. She absorbed the brokenness around her and began to believe it defined her. When we do this, the voice in our head begins shaping the way we live, often without us realizing it. We rehearse old wounds, replay past failures, and magnify fears until they loom larger than reality.

This is a deeply human pattern, but it's not the whole story. We need supernatural help from the Holy Spirit and the Holy Scriptures to heal our broken thinking, quiet the lies, and remind us who we truly are. His voice interrupts the noise, reframes our fears, and leads us toward freedom.

Let's return to Sheth's story and the woman who was trying to help him.

When the child's nurse heard the news, she picked him up and fled.

—2 Samuel 4:4c

Read 2 Samuel 4:4c in the margin. Who was this woman, and how was she trying to help Sheth?

A royal child like Mephibosheth would have been cared for by a *nurse* whose role wove together nurture, protection, and steady presence. She tended to his everyday needs, watched over his safety, and became a trusted figure within the household. Several Bible translations use words such as *nanny* or *caregiver* because they help us picture the warmth and responsibility wrapped into her role. As women, we recognize this rhythm of tending, guarding, and showing up with love.

Sheth's nurse imagined David to be an enemy, but David was different from other kings. This perceived threat wasn't real. Yet the moment she dropped Sheth, his body wasn't the only thing injured; his thinking surely was crippled too. Scripture tells us that she ran, responding instinctively to her fear. Sheth likely absorbed her fear, never questioning it; then he hid for years.

Can you think of a childhood fear that has shaped your thinking into adulthood? If so, write about it briefly.

When I was about Sheth's age, my bedroom doubled as the home for our old furnace—the kind that usually lives in a basement or garage. At its base, a three-foot strip of open flame burned steadily. My mom nightly reminded me to keep clothes and stuffed animals far from it.

Bedtime became a ritual of checking the furnace—once before lying down, then again each time I woke through the night. Eventually, a recurring nightmare took hold: I lay on a flying carpet in the pitch dark while flames licked upward around me. I woke drenched in sweat—sometimes multiple times each night. This nightmare pursued me long after childhood.

When I shared with my mom how this dream had been an unwelcome but familiar frenemy since childhood, she listened, prayed over me, and gently encouraged me to ask Jesus for His protection each night before bed. Following her tender wisdom helped, and the fiery nightmares ceased.

Sometimes we need professionals to help us in processing experiences and emotions. I am grateful to God for medical doctors, therapists, and others He uses to bring healing in our lives. God's desire for us is restoration and wholeness, which involves our thought patterns.

Read Romans 12:2 and Philippians 4:8 in the margin. How does God want to transform us?

> Let God transform you into a new person by changing the way you think.
>
> ***—Romans 12:2b***

What does God invite us to dwell on? List below the eight criteria that Paul shares in Philippians:

> Fix your thoughts on what is true, and honorable, and right, and pure, and lovely, and admirable. Think about things that are excellent and worthy of praise.
>
> ***—Philippians 4:8***

1. ____________________
2. ____________________
3. ____________________
4. ____________________
5. ____________________
6. ____________________
7. ____________________
8. ____________________

God wants to transform us by the renewing of our minds, and He invites us to dwell on the kinds of things that help shrink our fears in the light of His presence.

Most of my fears don't meet the first criterion. They are *not true.* The fear of sleeping near an open flame as a child was a valid fear, but the nightmare of being consumed by fire that accompanied me into adulthood was based in fear and was *not true.*

Paul's invitation in Philippians 4:8 is not a gentle suggestion; it is a reorientation of the mind. He is saying, in essence, "Aim your thoughts toward what is real, noble, and life-giving." When I do that, I notice how many of the internal thoughts I replay are neither true nor honorable. They are echoes of old wounds, misunderstandings, or imagined catastrophes. They feel *familiar,* but they are not *factual.*

If you carried the truth of Philippians 4:8 with you all week, how might it change your thinking?

Truth is not necessarily what our emotions are shouting in the moment—though our emotions can reveal something that is true within us. Discernment is needed to listen wisely and determine if a thought is true. Truth ultimately aligns with God's Word and character; it is always loving, wise, and good. When we fix our thoughts on God's truth, fear loses its authority. The anxious narratives quiet. The mind becomes a place where praise can breathe.

So a good question we can ask ourselves as we listen for Holy Spirit discernment is this: *Are the thoughts looping in my head actually true?* If not, with the Holy Spirit's help, we can release them. We can choose what is excellent. We can dwell on what is worthy of praise. And in that choosing, peace grows.

Truth is not necessarily what our emotions are shouting in the moment—though our emotions can reveal something that is true within us. Truth ultimately aligns with God's Word and character; it is always loving, wise, and good.

What are some thoughts looping in your head right now?

Are they true? Listen for the discernment of the Holy Spirit.

_____ Yes _____ No

What is something excellent and worthy of praise you can dwell on instead?

Reread this week's memory verse, Isaiah 53:5 The Voice, and fill in the blanks:

But he was __________ *because of us*; he suffered so.

Our __________ wounded and *crushed him*.

He endured the breaking that made us whole.

The injuries he suffered became our healing.

—Isaiah 53:5 *The Voice* (*emphasis added*)

Enter into a time of worship. Scan this QR code to listen to "You Say" by Lauren Daigle.

Write your name in the blank and let this become the blessing Jesus whispers over your heart.

My beloved ______________, I see where life has broken you—and I know how it twists your thoughts, making you feel less than and unseen. I did not come to condemn you but to lovingly restore you. Let Me reshape your thinking with what is true, honorable, and lovely. Fix your eyes on Me. I am the way that leads you out of fear and into freedom. I am the truth that silences every accusation. I am the life that breathes hope into your weary soul. You are Mine, and I am making all things new—even you.

Now offer your response: *Jesus, . . .*

Day 4: Broken World

Biblical Foundations:
2 Samuel 4:4d; 2 Chronicles 7:14

Focus Scripture:
(But as she hurried away, she dropped him, and he became crippled.)

—2 Samuel 4:4d

Yesterday we saw how internalizing our broken relationships, experiences, and fears can lead to broken thinking. Then we looked at how we can transform and overcome our broken thinking by following the instructions in Philippians 4:8.

Like Mephibosheth, we live in a scary, broken world that can cause us to retreat in fear. As the nightly news unveils the cracks in our world, we are reminded of our deep need for healing and restoration from One greater than ourselves, the only One strong enough to steady our trembling hearts.

Read 2 Samuel 4:4d in the margin. Circle the phrase that gives us a clue about why this accident might have happened. Draw one line under what Sheth's nurse did and two lines under what happened as a result.

(But as she hurried away, she dropped him, and he became crippled.)

—2 Samuel 4:4d

Accidents are more likely to happen when we are hurried and afraid. Understanding the nurse's fear helps us grasp how such a heartbreaking accident could occur. In the ancient world, a change in royal power often meant the family of the previous king was in danger. Even if the nation survived the invasion, the incoming king often would execute the former ruler's descendants to prevent any future claims to the throne. It was a time when changes in power brought peril rather than pageantry, risk rather than reverence.

Against that backdrop, Sheth's nanny had every reason to be afraid. When news of Saul and Jonathan's deaths reached her, she knew the child in her care could be in mortal danger. Today we're going to step back and look at the verses surrounding Sheth in the fourth chapter of 2 Samuel to give us further context.

When Ishbosheth, Saul's son, heard about Abner's death at Hebron, he lost all courage, and all Israel became paralyzed with fear.

—2 Samuel 4:1

Read 2 Samuel 4:1 in the margin. What do we learn from this verse?

Feel free to read the entirety of chapter 4 if you like, but fair warning—it's definitely rated R for violence. Here's a brief summary. The entire nation of Israel was paralyzed with fear. During this time, Saul's remaining son, Ishbosheth, was murdered in his sleep by two of his own guard captains. Believing they would earn David's favor, they brought him Ishbosheth's head as a reward. Instead, David condemned their actions and ordered their execution for committing a crime against Saul's family.

David knew God had already given him the throne. This posture is consistent with David's character throughout the opening chapters of 2 Samuel. Even after David was anointed the next king and was hunted by Saul, he never used force to seize the throne or to take Saul's life, despite multiple opportunities. David's restraint, humility, and confidence in God set the stage for the compassion he would show Sheth, a compassion that stands in stark contrast to the violent norms of his day.

What insights does this backstory give us related to the fear of Sheth's nurse?

Sheth's nurse likely heard about the violence and was understandably terrified. But instead of pausing to learn the truth—that David was actually protective of Saul's family—she reacted out of fear and fled in haste. Sheth's nanny reminds me of another woman in Scripture. Her name is Jehosheba.

Read 2 Kings 11:1-3. Who was Jehosheba, and what did she do?

These verses set the scene for all that happens in chapter 11. Though these violent events are not directly part of Mephibosheth's story, they are woven into the broken history of his nation unfolding around him—and they speak to us about confronting evil and making a difference in the face of fear. Feel free to read the entire chapter if you like, or here's another summary for you.

When King Ahaziah was killed, Jehosheba (King Ahaziah's sister) rescued her nephew (baby Joash) and hid him with his nurse in a bedroom in the temple. When the mother of King Ahaziah (Athaliah) learned her son was dead, she seized power by slaughtering all royal heirs—her own grandchildren.

For six years, Jehosheba hid young Joash while Queen Athaliah ruled. In the seventh year, the high priest Jehoiada (who also happened to be Jehosheba's husband) secretly gathered the temple guards and officials, revealed Joash, and armed them with strict orders to protect him.

On the sabbath, the guards took their positions. The high priest brought Joash out, crowned and anointed him, and the people shouted, "Long live the king!" Hearing the noise, Queen Athaliah rushed in, saw Joash by the pillar, and cried, "Treason!" Jehoiada ordered her removed, and her reign ended with her death at the palace gate.

Here, two women stood at opposite ends of life's spectrum. Queen Athaliah, the only woman to rule ancient Israel, was driven by fear and so consumed with protecting her position that she murdered her own grandchildren. In contrast, her half-sister, Jehosheba, used her position to protect Prince Joash, much as Sheth's nanny had protected him.

Jehosheba risked everything, choosing courage over comfort. While we may never face such drastic choices, we still live in a broken world. And like Sheth's nanny and Jehosheba, we have an active role to play as women of faith—to protect our young, to speak truth, and to nurture hope.

"If my people, who are called by my name, will humble themselves and pray and seek my face and turn from their wicked ways, then I will hear from heaven, and I will forgive their sin and ***will heal their land.***"

—2 Chronicles 7:14 NIV (emphasis added)

Read 2 Chronicles 7:14 in the margin and circle three things this verse tells us to do.

God invites us first to humble our hearts before Him—letting go of pride, hurry, and self-reliance—so He can lift and empower us. Without Him, we can do nothing lasting. Second, He calls us to pray and seek His face with intention and longing, drawing close to Him who provides clarity and peace. And third, He urges us to turn from anything that pulls us away from Him, choosing His way so healing can flow into our lives, our families, and our land.

Like Sheth's nurse and Jehosheba, how can you use your influence—however quiet or hidden—to preserve life, truth, and hope?

Though we live in a broken world, God does *not* want us to live in fear. My hope for each of us is that we will continually draw near to Him so we may receive what we need to become courageous conduits of His love and healing in our world.

Reread this week's memory verse and fill in the blanks:

But he was _______ *because of us;* he suffered so.

Our __________ wounded and *crushed him.*

He endured the__________ that made us whole.

The injuries he suffered became our healing.

—Isaiah 53:5 *The Voice (emphasis added)*

Write your name in the blank and let this become the blessing Jesus whispers over your heart.

My beloved______________, I know this broken world can feel frightening—even paralyzing—yet in the face of fear, you can turn to Me and the truth I've given you. Like Jehosheba and Mephibosheth's nurse, you are a protector of promise and a defender of the innocent. I've placed within you courage to speak and step forward when fear says "stay hidden." You are not forgotten, powerless, or alone. I am your strength and your voice when you feel vulnerable. You are mine, beloved—and I am with you.

Now offer your response: *Jesus, . . .*

Enter into a time of worship. Scan this QR code to listen to "Oceans (Where Feet May Fail)" by Hillsong UNITED.

Day 5: Broken Spirit

Biblical Foundation:
Psalm 34:18; Romans 8:26; 1 John 4:18

Focus Scripture:
The LORD is close to the brokenhearted;
he rescues those whose spirits are crushed. —Psalm 34:18

Thank you for your perseverance and courage as we've navigated hard places together this week. Living in a broken world often distracts and discourages us from pushing forward. Dwelling on all that has happened in the past or could go wrong in the future can burden and break our spirits.

I believe this is what happened to Mephibosheth. As the grandson of Saul, he likely believed David's throne spelled danger for him. Despite knowing that David had not dealt harshly with any of Saul's descendants, Sheth remained in hiding. It seems that fear kept him distant from the time he was five until he was a man. Understandably, Sheth's broken body, broken relationships, broken thinking, and broken world must have led to a broken spirit.

We can observe this pattern in our own lives too. Fear immobilizes us. We stop looking at facts and let fear dominate, becoming stuck in patterns of hiding. This is why it's essential for us to dwell in our King's love. We can then make decisions that are not driven by fear but are informed and influenced by love. One of my favorite verses gently reminds us of this truth.

Such love has no fear, because perfect love expels all fear. If we are afraid, it is for fear of punishment, and this shows that we have not fully experienced his perfect love.
—1 John 4:18

Read 1 John 4:18 in the margin. Underline the words *no* and *all,* letting the truth of this statement bring peace to your soul. What is one practical way you could apply this truth in your life this week?

Mephibosheth feared punishment despite his innocence, trapped in circumstances beyond his control.

When have you feared punishment though you had done nothing wrong?

Like Sheth, we all carry fears—often born from wounds that left their mark. When I was sixteen, I was in a high-speed auto crash. It was my first solo trip driving out of town, and my dad had bestowed me the keys to our one roadworthy family vehicle. Feeling very grown-up, I had permission to attend a youth event in a small town located a few hours away from our farming community.

While driving home on the narrow two-lane highway, my front passenger tire slipped into the rut where the road had been widened and patched. I panicked, and panic did what panic does best—it took the wheel. At sixty miles an hour, the car snapped into a wild fishtail. A huge sedan barreled toward me.

To the right of this narrow highway stretched a deep ravine with a railroad track on the ridge beyond it. A head-on collision seemed certain. With no power steering, I threw my weight into cranking the wheel left, slamming my shoulder against the driver's-side door.

Only after crashing did I realize this maneuver had sent me careening straight into a brand-new car dealership. You have my permission to giggle—because if you're going to lose control of a vehicle, you might as well aim for the place with the newest cars!

Like a billiard ball ricocheting across a pool table, my family's stripped-down Maverick grazed five brightly colored trucks lined up on the front row of the dealership. Until that moment, I had never set foot on a new-car lot and had no idea that the most expensive vehicles were displayed up front.

After grazing five trucks and two cars, my family's car finally spun out and stalled, coming to rest beside a pristine white sedan—far nicer than our green Maverick, which now looked like a crumpled 7UP can.

I was dazed and bruised but, miraculously—unlike Sheth—could walk away from the accident. The driver's-side door was mangled, so I crawled out the passenger side. The dealership owner came running—absolutely delighted, explaining he had just sold seven vehicles in seven seconds. It was his best day of sales all month. His exuberance only deepened my humiliation.

People eating in the restaurant next door began drifting outside to witness the wreckage. I limped toward the owner's office to use the phone. Cell phones didn't exist back then, so I dialed my parents from the rotary phone on his desk. When I heard my mom's voice, I started to sob uncontrollably. I managed to share the address of where I was, but I couldn't find the courage to share all the details—seven large, crumpled details, to be exact.

My family was poor. All I could think was that my college tuition lay scattered across the lot. I had been saving for university for as long as I could remember. At sixteen, I was certain I had just ruined my future. When a policeman arrived and requested my insurance papers, I froze. Never once had I thought about insurance—but of course, my father, who worked three jobs, had me covered.

The officer asked if I was *fine,* then he handed me a *fine*—a fifty-dollar ticket. The irony was that my dad drove an old truck he'd bought for fifty dollars from a man from our church. My dad always used to say that "new cars make poor investments," so you can imagine his shock when he picked up his middle child from the middle of a wrecked car lot. I remember feeling so sorry and shaken. The goose egg on the side of my head eventually went down, the bruises faded, and the whiplash healed, but even now, when I'm driving on unfamiliar highways—especially in the dark or bad weather—fear can still bubble up.

I share this so that you know you are not alone if driving stirs anxiety or fear in you. Even if you've never plowed through a new-car lot, you may carry your own memories of white-knuckled moments behind the wheel.

When fear visits me, I picture Jesus sitting beside me—steady, present, loving me right in the middle of my shakiness. Sometimes I turn on a Christian radio station and let the music loosen my grip on the wheel. Other times, I simply whisper the name of Jesus. The Holy Spirit meets me in my weakness, just as Romans 8:26 promises. I inhale peace and exhale fear as I repeat His name—the One who calms storms both outside and within.

Read Romans 8:26 in the margin and paraphrase the promise in your own words below. Where do you feel this promise settling—in your mind, your chest, or your gut?

And the Holy Spirit helps us in our weakness. For example, we don't know what God wants us to pray for. But the Holy Spirit prays for us with groanings that cannot be expressed in words.

—Romans 8:26

Paul's word *weakness* in this verse points to our human limitations that leave us unable to articulate what we need. It names those moments when our thoughts are tangled, our emotions feel too heavy to carry, and our prayers dissolve into silence because we don't know where to begin.

In those places, the Spirit doesn't shame us. The Spirit comes alongside us, holding what we cannot hold and speaking what we cannot speak. Our weakness becomes the very place where God meets us—not because the struggle itself is good, but because God refuses to leave us alone in it.

Though prayer and the name of Jesus hold real power, it is important to remember that trauma affects the nervous system in ways that God often heals through the care of trained professionals. Seeking help when anxiety or fear becomes debilitating is not a lack of faith—it is wisdom, courage, and stewardship of the body and mind God entrusted to us. God works through therapists, doctors, and trusted helpers too.

I can look back now and laugh about the day I accidentally played billiards with the family sedan in a brand-new-car lot. But some struggles aren't funny, and some seasons leave us feeling like a puddle of tears. Even then, God doesn't ask us to pretend. He simply stands ready to steady us, breathe for us, and guide us toward the help we need.

Without the Spirit's strength, none of us could live the life God calls us to. But with the Spirit—quietly interceding, gently strengthening, faithfully accompanying—we discover that we are never too broken, never abandoned, and never beyond hope. Even in our most fragile moments, God is nurturing something tender and true in us: the assurance that we are held, loved, and never alone.

The LORD is close to the brokenhearted;
he rescues those whose spirits are crushed.
—*Psalm 34:18*

Read Psalm 34:18 in the margin. What part of your body relaxes when you read this promise?

Like Sheth, who lived in fear for decades with a broken spirit, I can tell you firsthand of God's faithfulness to rescue us. We are never alone. His Spirit breathes courage into our steps, even on days when brokenness feels heavy. We are loved by our heavenly Father. Truly "the LORD is close to the brokenhearted; he rescues those whose spirits are crushed."

Enter into a time of worship. Scan this QR code to listen to "Worn" by Tenth Avenue North.

Reread this week's memory verse and fill in the blanks:

But he was ________ *because of us;* he suffered so.

Our ________ wounded and *crushed him.*

He endured the ________ ***that made us whole.***

The injuries he suffered became our ________.

—Isaiah 53:5 *The Voice (emphasis added)*

Write your name in the blank and let this become the blessing Jesus whispers over your heart.

My beloved ________________, I have seen the years when fear pressed hard against your spirit, though none of it was your fault. I have never stepped away. I draw close to the brokenhearted and save those who feel crushed inside. Bring Me the fears that whisper to you in the night—the fear of accidents, of not being enough, of rejection, of the future. You were never meant to carry these alone. Place them in My hands. Rest in My nearness. Let My peace steady you. I am restoring what fear has taken and breathing new strength into you even now.

Now offer your response: *Jesus, . . .*

Week 1

Video Viewer Guide

1. When I look at ______-phib-o-sheth, I see the first two letters.

   I see__________.

2. Trials are simply a __________ _____ __________ in a world that's broken.

   And in the middle of it all, Jesus offers us ____________that does not depend on circumstances.

3. The Greek word *teleios* means perfect, ______________—not flawless.

4. We're not to rejoice ________________of the trials. We're to rejoice in what those trials can __________________.

5. Though not everything in life_____ ____________, God lovingly gathers every thread and works them together_______ _______ ____________ of those who trust Him.

6. Our own scars don't disqualify us—they mark us as___________________.

WEEK 2

Experiencing Loneliness and Isolation

Memory Verse

"Do not be afraid or discouraged, for the Lord *will personally go ahead of you. He will be with you; he will neither fail you nor abandon you."*

—Deuteronomy 31:8

Recipe of the Week

The secret to the *most perfect* banana bread is to use the *most imperfect* bananas! I seek out bananas that some would discard because they're too blemished and imperfect. This recipe has the least amount of oil and refined sugar because it uses four large bananas. Go bananas and double the recipe. It freezes beautifully and is even moister after defrosting. You'll have extra on hand to bless a neighbor!

Introduction to This Week

2 Samuel 9:1-5

Last week we met Mephibosheth—a boy born a prince, positioned to inherit his grandfather's throne. But everything changed the day Saul and Jonathan died in battle. At just five years old, he lost his father and grandfather, his health, and his promising future. One fall left him physically broken, and no doubt his thinking followed. He grew up limping, hiding in a fear-warped world that no doubt resulted in a deeply wounded spirit. This week we'll see that Sheth's story has threads that are woven throughout our own stories. We, too, have times when we feel like we have fallen from favor and need to hide our hurts.

Day 1: Wanting Favor

Biblical Foundations:
1 Samuel 20:14-17; 2 Samuel 9:1; Mark 5:25-34

Focus Scripture:
One day David asked, "Is anyone in Saul's family still alive—anyone to whom I can show kindness for Jonathan's sake?" —2 Samuel 9:1

I can still vividly remember my first day of public high school after eight years in a Christian school. Like every freshman girl, I longed to find favor and make friends. Wanting to look my best, I chose a lavender blouse adorned with delicate Swiss polka dots and paired it with a cream skirt.

I'd never had a locker or a homeroom before, so naturally I was concerned about finding both. By the time I located my desk in first period, I was sweaty but blamed my nerves and the lack of air-conditioning. As I sat in homeroom, I noticed my legs felt damp—but I had *no clue* that something truly torrential was underway. I was beginning my very first menstrual cycle. (You have permission to *gasple*—that unthinkable gasp-giggle combo.)

When the bell rang, I trekked back to my locker two hallways away, feeling proud for bravely navigating this new, chaotic world. When I bent down to grab my books, my dear friend Susie floated up behind me and delivered the shocking news. The back of my skirt looked like a crime scene. My cheeks were probably the same shade.

On the very day I hoped to make a splash and win new friends, I certainly gained attention—just not in the way I intended. Susie shielded me from embarrassment, walking behind me to block the view of my soiled skirt. She lived just down the alley from me and compassionately followed me all the way home. There, my mom gently consoled me as I sobbed that I wanted to hide forever. Then she took me shopping for a new pair of jeans—a safer wardrobe option for the next day of school.

Maybe you didn't have your first period during your first day of high school while wearing a cream skirt, but you likely have experienced other moments when you felt like you fell from favor. Maybe you were once the favorite child until a few poor decisions altered how your family saw you. Maybe you never felt important or pretty. Perhaps it started when you were chosen last on the playground or in PE class, always on the outside because you wore secondhand clothes—and everyone knew it. Perhaps others looked down on you and assumed you weren't bright simply because you lived in the wrong neighborhood or your parents drove the wrong car. (I can relate to all of these.)

Regardless of socioeconomic class, if you've ever had a teenager, you know what it feels like to fall from favor. Suddenly, they favor their friends over their folks. They roll their eyes and pronounce your name with a newfound disdain: "Motherrrrrrrrrrrrr." (Can you hear it?) Once, their eyes lit up when you called their name. Now, they don't answer your calls or texts until they're bored and have nothing better to do. They want freedom, and your existence feels like a threat to their independence. They need you, but they don't want you. (God knows how it feels when children come only when they need something.)

Maybe you've fallen from favor at your workplace. The new witty employee with fewer years of experience and far less sweat equity gets the promotion you were promised. Or maybe your company "rightsized," downsizing you right out of a paycheck. Human Resources says it's *nothing personal.*

Maybe you've fallen from favor with friends and suddenly find yourself the odd gal out for no apparent reason. No one notices you're missing at their gatherings. You only see the pictures online afterward—everyone smiling, everyone together—and somehow you feel more alone than ever.

We've all had misunderstandings with friends. Sometimes words spoken behind our backs make their way to our ears and adhere to our tender hearts like Velcro. Some hurts leave scars long after forgiveness is extended. Friends shouldn't be fickle, but at times their favor shifts like the wind. Time passes, silence grows, and distance settles in.

Falling from favor feels a lot like being dropped. When your insurance company drops you because you're *high risk*, it feels personal. When your phone call is dropped at an odd moment in the conversation, it can feel like you've been hung up on. And we all can relate to that age-old experience when you're connecting with a friend or a romantic interest and suddenly—poof—they drop you and disappear. Today we call it being ghosted.

Life holds disappointments—some small, some life-changing.

Which of the preceding examples resonates most strongly with you, and why?

Mephibosheth knew what it was like to be dropped. He understood what it felt like to fall from favor. He grew from a boy into a man who likely needed crutches in a world where walking was the primary mode of transportation. There was no Disability Act ensuring ramps, restrooms, or equal employment opportunities. If you were disabled like Sheth, you likely had no way to provide for your family other than begging. He must have felt as though his future held little hope.

While Sheth's life may have seemed devoid of blessing, David's was overflowing with royal blessing. His first twenty years as king were marked by unity, expansion, and God's unmistakable favor. Israel stood united, with Jerusalem firmly established as its capital and surrounding enemy nations subdued.

As David's wealth increased and loyal leaders gathered around him, his reign grew in stability, strength, and international respect. These were the golden years of David's rule, and this is the backdrop for our Scripture Focus today.

Reread today's Scripture Focus, 2 Samuel 9:1 (page 49). What does David's question reveal about his heart?

One of David's shining moments—when he most resembled a man after God's own heart (1 Samuel 13:14)—is rooted in this inquiry. King David's covenant love toward Jonathan extended to Jonathan's son, Sheth, and reminds us of the kind of love our King has toward us.

David remembered his covenant that we learned about on Day 1.

Summarize 1 Samuel 20:14-17 in your own words below:

Mephibosheth was a prince who lost his health and his position, being relegated to lonely obscurity. This reminds me of a similar person whose story is so important that we find it in all three Synoptic Gospels.

Read Mark 5:25-34 and summarize in your own words this beautiful encounter between Jesus and a shunned woman in need. What stands out most to you?

Perhaps as comforting as the healing itself was the tender name Jesus spoke to this woman who had suffered for twelve years. He called her *daughter*—the only time in all of Scripture He used this particular term of endearment.

The timing tells me that this was no casual accident. Jesus was on His way to heal the twelve-year-old daughter of a respected synagogue leader, making this the only intertwined miracle in all of Scripture. Two daughters, two stories, two very opposite places in society: one shunned as unclean and treated as a nuisance, the other cherished and honored by her community.

If you remember nothing else from today's lesson, let it be this: no matter what you say about yourself or what others have thought or spoken about you, Jesus calls you His *daughter*. He is not too busy, too preoccupied, or too overwhelmed with more "important" people to make time and space for you. He wants to see you.

What tender place in your heart most needs to hear this truth right now? What fear, loss, or hope is held there?

Jesus wants you to come close because He longs to touch you, lift your hurts, quiet your fears, ease your loneliness, and restore your life. Don't let the world's busyness or the voices of others drown out His voice. Regardless of stigma or status, health or wealth, past or present, you are His beloved daughter now and forever.

Reread this week's memory verse:

> "*Do not be afraid or discouraged, for the* LORD *will personally go ahead of you. He will be with you; he will neither fail you nor abandon you.*"
>
> —Deuteronomy 31:8

Write your name in the blank and let this become the blessing Jesus whispers over your heart.

My beloved ________________, come close to Me. I see the wounds you've carried for so long, the labels others have placed on you, the whispers that have tried to define your worth. But none of those voices speaks truth. I call you daughter—cherished, chosen, and seen. As I paused for the woman who reached for My robe, I pause for you. Draw near, for I long to lift your hurt, quiet your fear, and restore your life. Let no noise of this world drown out My love. You are, now and forever, My beloved.

Now offer your response: *Jesus, . . .*

Enter into a time of worship. Scan this QR code to listen to "Not for a Moment (After All)" by Meredith Andrews.

Day 2: Wearing the Cloak of Shame

Biblical Foundations:

Joshua 2; 2 Samuel 9:2-3; John 10:10; 2 Corinthians 5:17-20; 7:10; 1 John 1:9

Focus Scripture:

He summoned a man named Ziba, who had been one of Saul's servants. "Are you Ziba?" the king asked.

"Yes sir, I am," Ziba replied.

The king then asked him, "Is anyone still alive from Saul's family? If so, I want to show God's kindness to them."

Ziba replied, "Yes, one of Jonathan's sons is still alive. He is crippled in both feet."

—2 Samuel 9:2-3

Yesterday I shared the infamous story of starting my period on the first day of high school while wearing a cream-colored skirt. Maybe you've had a similar menstrual mishap that left you embarrassed and wanting to hide. But some of the accidents in our lives run deeper. Some come from painful experiences, unexpected losses, or even choices we regret—moments with heavier, more lasting repercussions. When we hide our imperfections and retreat into low places, we often trade our identity in Christ and our robe of righteousness for a cloak of shame.

Like Mephibosheth, many of us learn at a young age to drape ourselves in labels that were never ours to wear. Instead of seeing God's truth, our past whispers that we are broken or bad. We wear labels that don't reflect who we are in Christ—such as divorcée, bad mom, too much, not enough, or countless others.

A glance in the mirror can trigger self-loathing words like *stupid*, *ugly*, *fat*, or *clumsy*. Harsh names spill out—names we would never dream of speaking over anyone else. Nevertheless, we cloak ourselves with them. We may never verbalize these names in public, but make no mistake, we whisper these names over ourselves in private darkness.

What are some of the labels or critical words that seem to cover you?

Our tendency to hide in shame began back in the garden of Eden when our sister Eve believed the lie that God was withholding good from her. The moment she ate the fruit, she felt exposed and ashamed (Genesis 3:1-7). But God has never withheld good from His daughters. He withholds nothing except what would harm us or keep us from our ultimate good.

Please believe this with your whole heart.

Just as God sought out Eve and her husband when they hid in the garden, He calls us out of our own hiding places. He does not disgrace our nakedness or our brokenness. Instead, He tenderly provides coverings. In Eden, He replaced Adam and Eve's self-made fig leaves—destined to dry out, crack, and scratch—with durable, soft skins that required the death of a living creature (Genesis 3:21). Through Jesus's death and resurrection, He offers us something far greater than Eden's temporary coverings—robes of righteousness! (See Isaiah 61:10; 2 Corinthians 5:21; and Ephesians 4:24.)

Just as our King calls us out of hiding—often through those who serve Him—King David summoned a servant named Ziba to help call Sheth out of hiding.

He withholds nothing except what would harm us or keep us from our ultimate good.

Reread today's Focus Scripture, 2 Samuel 9:2-3 (page 54). Write the servant's response to David's inquiry below, including the last sentence.

This last line breaks my heart: "He is crippled in both feet." Given that David had already said he wanted "to show [him] God's kindness," why did Ziba feel the need to add this? His comment gives us a glimpse into his mindset. For Ziba—and for many in the ancient world—physical disability often carried stigma. People with visible limitations were frequently judged, pitied, or even assumed to have brought misfortune upon themselves. By emphasizing Mephibosheth's condition, Ziba reveals more about his own assumptions than about Sheth's worth.

Each mention of Sheth's disability underscores that he was "crippled in both feet." The world underscores our own deficiencies as well. Yet despite what the world may think, whisper, or shout about our broken places, we are never too damaged for our King. He is compassionate. He sees the weight of being broken, and yet He moves toward us with healing, dignity, and love.

While some commentators assume Sheth's legs were physically broken when he was dropped, and then healing incorrectly and leaving him lame, others suggest the injury was a permanent spinal cord injury. Either way, the shame placed on him by a society that looked down on the sick and disabled—often labeling them unclean—must have been even more debilitating.

Thankfully, God doesn't leave us alone in our brokenness. He is a good Father. Mephibosheth also had a good father in Jonathan, who first gave him the name of Merib-baal, which means "beloved of the lord" in Hebrew[1]—and which later was changed to *Mephibosheth* for reasons we'll learn in week 6. In Hebrew, Mephibosheth means "shame destroyer." The first part comes from the verb meaning to break apart, and the second part is from the noun for shame.[2]

While Jonathan didn't know what Sheth would face in his lifetime, God certainly did. I believe this is one of the reasons God chose to preserve Sheth's story for us. God does not want us to limp under the burden of shame. God wants to "destroy shame" in our lives.

When in your story have you felt pulled into the shadow of shame, even for a moment? What happened?

What did you need in that moment that you didn't receive?

I once had a math teacher who poisoned her young students with shame. Whenever someone committed what she deemed an infraction, she would glare them down, squint her eyes, and wag her head. Then she would peer over her large bosom with her double chin, making her look doubly powerful. She pointed her finger like it was a magic wand and she was placing a curse on you. Then she spewed three dreadful words: "Shame on you." This seemed to be her favorite phrase when she was annoyed. I dreaded her class and disliked math after that experience. Looking back now, I am sorry she chose to be a teacher, leaving a legacy of shame.

Thankfully, my parents encouraged me, building me up so I could bounce back from someone who shamed me. Not every student has that firm foundation. Some kids are fed a steady diet of shame. It's no wonder their self-worth is malnourished, too anemic to endure life's hardships. If you were shamed as a child, please know that our King does not shame you. He cherishes you. He promises to care for you.

Look up 2 Corinthians 5:17-20. If this scripture had a scent, sound, or texture, what would it be for you?

Though God never shames us, He did create us with a conscience to call us home when we stray. The Bible tells us that even unbelievers have God's law written on their hearts and instinctively know right from wrong because they have a conscience to guide them (Romans 2:14-15). Our consciences allow us to feel guilt, but guilt is different from shame.

Shame	**Guilt**
Shame is focused on the person.	Guilt is focused on the action.
Shame says you are unforgivable.	Guilt says return to God for forgiveness.
Shame is debilitating.	Guilt is liberating when we turn to God.
Shame says I did something bad; therefore, I am bad.	Guilt says the sin is bad.

For the kind of sorrow God wants us to experience leads us away from sin and results in salvation. There's no regret for that kind of sorrow. But worldly sorrow, which lacks repentance, results in spiritual death.

—2 Corinthians 7:10

Read 2 Corinthians 7:10 in the margin. Underline the first sentence. Draw a line through the last sentence.

The first sentence describes godly *guilt.* The last sentence describes ungodly *shame.* Grace gives shame an eviction notice!

Grace gives shame an eviction notice!

If we confess our sins to him, he is faithful and just to forgive us our sins and to cleanse us from all wickedness.

—1 John 1:9

Read 1 John 1:9 in the margin. Imagine Jesus speaking this directly to you. What word or phrase stands out?

Now draw an anchor in the margin below the verse.

This promise can serve as a beautiful anchor to secure us when we are tossed with guilt and are longing for assurance of God's mercy. When we ask God to forgive us, He is faithful and just. He not only forgives us but also purifies us. We don't need to feel shame because we are cleansed by the blood of Jesus! When grace walks in, shame needs to make like a tree and leave!

The thief's purpose is to steal and kill and destroy. My purpose is to give them a rich and satisfying life.

—*John 10:10*

Read John 10:10 in the margin and look at the image. Which door is Jesus holding open? Write his name above it.

Jesus said that He came so that we can experience life to the fullest. He tells us that Satan came to "steal and kill and destroy." Satan, the Accuser, can take something that can be used for good, guilt, and twist it so that it is used for bad, shame. But God does just the opposite. Romans 8:28 tells us that He can take something that is bad and use it for good. Take heart, my friend. This means He can bring good from the bad decisions we have made. Our King redeems both us and the things we have done.

If you still carry even a twinge of doubt, let me comfort you with what I'll call "The Rehab of Rahab," found in Joshua 2.

Read Joshua 2. What label was given to Rahab?

Rahab lived with the unwanted label of a prostitute. (Remember, labels are not who we are or how God sees us!) In her humility, she allowed her low status to become a doorway for God's higher plan—a reminder that God brings redemption and purpose to anyone who comes to Him.

When God's people conquered Jericho, Rahab and her family were protected. Her forwarding address is noteworthy. She moved from a house of shame (Joshua 2) to the faith hall of fame (Hebrews 11). Aside from Sarah—the matriarch of our Christian faith—Rahab is the only other woman named in this elite list! Even more noteworthy, Matthew includes her as one of the five women in Christ's royal lineage (Matthew 1:5), living proof that God does not allow shame to have the final word!

So when regret rings your doorbell, trying to sell you a heavy coat of shame, send Jesus to answer the door. In the glow of God's presence, you have no use for shame's cloak. It serves no purpose other than to weigh you down and make you sweat miserably.

Remember, Mephibosheth means "shame destroyer." His story can erase the shame in our story. Shame that cripples us can be replaced by grace that frees us!

Enter into a time of worship. Scan this QR code to listen to "Rescue" by Lauren Daigle.

Reread this week's memory verse and fill in the blank:

"Do not be _______ or discouraged, for the LORD will personally go ahead of you. He will be with you; he will neither fail you nor abandon you."

—Deuteronomy 31:8

Write your name in the blank and let this become the blessing Jesus whispers over your heart.

My beloved_______________, come to Me and lay down the cloak of shame you've worn for far too long. Let Me remove every negative label, every accusing thought, every whisper that contradicts My truth. Receive instead the radiant robe of My righteousness—light, lovely, and pure. Rest in My cleansing love that washes you new each moment. Fix your gaze on Me. Walk with Me in the freedom I purchased for you, clothed in grace, covered in mercy, cherished beyond measure.

Now offer your response: Jesus, . . .

Day 3: Living in Lo-debar

Biblical Foundations:
Genesis 16:1-6, 13a-b; 2 Samuel 9:4a

Focus Scripture:
"Where is he?" the king asked.

"In Lo-debar," Ziba told him. —2 Samuel 9:4a

Yesterday we learned the important differences between guilt and shame. Shame is focused on the person. Guilt is focused on the action. Sheth did nothing wrong. He had no reason to feel shame. Like Sheth, sometimes we have done nothing wrong yet we feel shame. Even if we made a mistake and sinned, our King doesn't want us to wear the cloak of shame. He doesn't want us to hide from Him. King David didn't want Sheth to hide from him either, which is why he asked this important question. Listen to the answer he received.

"Where is he?" the king asked.

"In Lo-debar," Ziba told him.

—2 Samuel 9:4a

Read 2 Samuel 9:4a in the margin. Underline what King David asked, and circle the response.

If you want a glimpse inside our King's heart, look at David's response when he learned that Sheth was crippled. He didn't ask, "How broken is he?" Instead, he asked, "Where is he?" Likewise, our King doesn't ask, "How broken are you?" Instead, He asks, "Where are you?"

"Come to me, all of you who are weary and carry heavy burdens, and I will give you rest."

—Matthew 11:28

Read Matthew 11:28 in the margin. Describe how it feels knowing you too have a King who asks for your presence, not your perfection.

This invitation is not based on how good we are but on how good God is. We each have places we hide when we feel broken and vulnerable. When I was young, I would hide outside my mom's kitchen window in the playhouse my dad made. There I would imagine life to be perfect.

Like Sheth, we often hide in low, lonely places like Lo-debar. Lo-debar comes from the Hebrew *lo*, meaning "no" or "not." It's paired with *debar*, meaning "pasture."[3] When put together, the name paints a picture of a place that means "the land of no pasture." It was the land of nothing—basically, ancient Israel's version of "the middle of nowhere." Lo-debar was a land of forgotten things, where broken dreams and broken people could hide.

Scripture often lets geography preach. Lo-debar becomes more than a dot on an ancient map; it becomes a living metaphor for the seasons when our souls feel barren, silent, or spiritually dried up. And in God's hands, even desolate places can become staging grounds for grace. Suddenly, the dusty map turns into a tender picture of the journey from fear to favor.

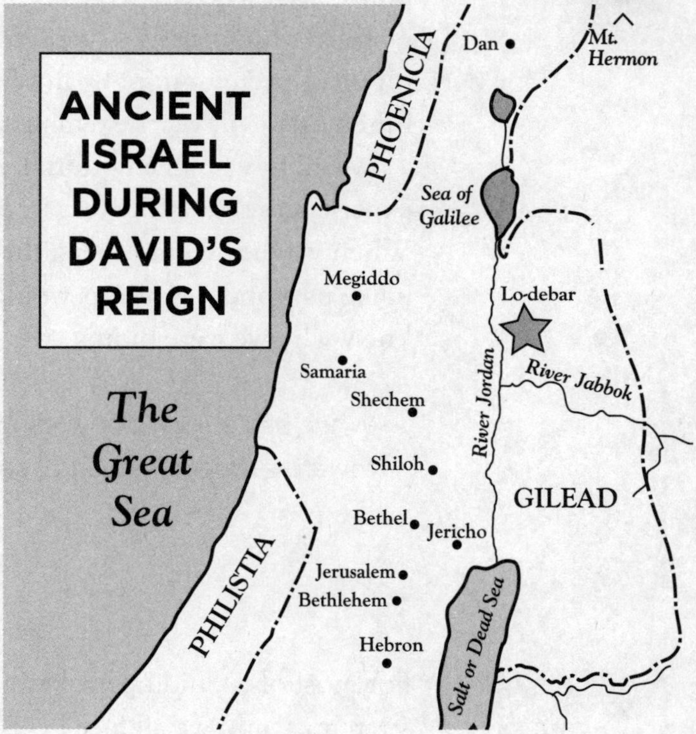

Believing King David meant him harm, Sheth hid for years in that lonely land of Lo-debar. We recognize that place too—the inner wilderness we retreat to when pain feels too heavy to name. His story gently invites us to acknowledge our own tender places, those corners of the heart where we long for favor.

Instead of listening to our King and turning to His Word for direction, we often withdraw. Fear whispers that we've fallen from favor—that if others saw our brokenness, they would turn away. So we shrink back, hiding in low and lonely places. But even there, God sees us. His grace reaches into the shadows, calling us out of hiding with a kindness that does not rush or shame.

What is your familiar Lo-debar, and when do you find yourself most tempted to hide there?

We each seek relief differently. Perhaps you hide in your bed scrolling on your phone. Maybe you retreat to the couch to binge-watch TV. Some soothe stress with online shopping while others slip into their pantry and eat. I've done all of these at one time or another.

Some find that alcohol mutes the voices in their heads. As a former pharmacist who has lived through the opioid epidemic—now deepened by the fentanyl crisis—I've seen how prescription drugs can dull both physical and emotional pain. Food, alcohol, and medications aren't inherently evil, yet the tempter can twist them into traps.

We all have had emotional, spiritual, and perhaps even physical experiences that strike fear in our hearts and lead us to hide in Lo-debar. When we hide from others, this can trigger feelings of loneliness. It can make us wonder if others would think less of us, or truly love us, if they knew why we were hiding.

When has pulling away resulted in a heaviness of spirit, pressing you toward sadness instead of safety?

For most of us, hiding brokenness makes life heavier. Some seasons truly stretch us, and we all face Lo-debar moments, especially when family isn't close. In our highly mobile culture, we Americans often live far from the kind of support systems previous generations relied on. Mobility may be normal, but it can leave us vulnerable, navigating hard seasons without the steady presence of generational care.

Sometimes we choose to live in loneliness. Other times, the journey is forced upon us. Either way, it reminds me of Hagar's tender story.

Read Genesis 16:1-7 and summarize it in your own words below.

What happens in verse 7 makes my soul sing! Our King sought out Hagar and found her in the wilderness. Do you see the parallel? This is what King David did for Sheth. Just as Hagar ran away, Sheth ran away. We run away too. But we don't need to because our King wants us to run to Him. David looked for Sheth, and God looks for us, just as He looked for Hagar.

Read Genesis 16:13a-b in the margin. How did Hagar refer to God?

Thereafter, Hagar used another name to refer to the LORD, who had spoken to her. She said, "You are the God who sees me."

—Genesis 16:13a-b

Does any part of Hagar's story feel like an invitation to breathe again—to rest in God's attentive care? Explain your response.

The Hebrew name for "the God who sees me" is El Roi—the God who sees the overlooked, the wounded, and the wandering. Friend, God's gaze is never distant or indifferent. In every Lo-debar moment, He notices, understands, and moves with compassion, reminding you that you are not ever invisible to Him.

Enter into a time of worship. Scan this QR code to listen to "Run to the Father" by Cody Carnes.

Reread this week's memory verse and fill in the blanks.

"Do not be __________ or discouraged, for the ______ will personally go ahead of you. He will be with you; he will neither fail you nor abandon you."

—Deuteronomy 31:8

Write your name in the blank and let this become the blessing Jesus whispers over your heart.

My beloved ________________, I see you in the hidden places where your heart retreats, the quiet corners that feel like Lo-debar—empty, barren, far from hope. You do not need to stay there. Come to Me. Do not seek comfort in eating, scrolling, shopping, or numbing with drink; these are broken cisterns that cannot hold what your soul longs for. Let My presence soothe your weariness and quiet the cravings that rise within. Draw near, and I will meet you with tenderness. You are Mine.

Now offer your response: *Jesus, . . .*

Day 4: Hiding Hurts

Biblical Foundations:
2 Samuel 9:4b; Matthew 11:28-30; 2 Corinthians 4:8-9

Focus Scripture:
Ziba told him, "at the home of Makir son of Ammiel." —2 Samuel 9:4b

My daughter's huge hazel eyes looked up at me in shock. She was pinned underneath a metal cart filled with groceries on the floor of the cereal aisle at the supermarket. The front bar of the lower rack awkwardly forced her chin backward. Her sweet, almost-seven-year-old hands gripped the bar that pressed against her windpipe.

It all happened so fast. One minute she was gazing upward in hope, staring at the box of sweet Cap'n Crunch cereal, and the next minute her little brother came barreling down the aisle full speed. She turned toward him.

Bang!

She was being dragged under the cart like a Swiffer mop. Garrett couldn't begin to see over the cart. At five, he was full of boundless energy, racing like he was in the Indianapolis 500. I chased him, screaming. "STOP! You've run over your sister!"

A stock boy hurried toward me to help, as I instinctively lifted the loaded cart to free my little girl. She was wedged perfectly between the two front wheels. Her chin kept the cart from running over her completely—and removing her pudgy little nose in the process.

I asked the normal mommy questions like, "Are you hurt?" She had just one question for me: "Mom, just this once, could we buy Cap'n Crunch?"

This story still makes me laugh—and cry, because it happened during one of the scariest months of my life. It all started when I palpated a lump during a breast self-exam. I'd love to tell you that I was unwavering with my rock-solid faith, but I was terrified. My first thoughts were about my little ones.

My husband worked ridiculously long hours, sometimes fourteen days in a row. Who would read them stories, say prayers, and tuck them in bed if something happened to me? By the end of the following week, my gynecologist had worked me in and attempted a needle biopsy. The lump was large. She couldn't aspirate any fluid, which was a bad sign.

So she sent me to the hospital to make an appointment with the interventional radiologist for a biopsy. During the weeks of waiting for the appointment and then the pathology report, I felt dazed—like I was pinned under a grocery cart being dragged along a concrete floor.

During that time, I bartered with God, praying, "If you will just let this not be cancer and let me raise my children, I'll never ask for anything else." Bartering isn't uncommon when we're desperate.

Reread today's Focus Scripture, 2 Samuel 9:4b (page 67). In whose home was Mephibosheth living?

Mephibosheth hid for years in the home of Makir, whose name means "bartered."[4] It makes me wonder what Sheth bartered to buy protection from a man named "bartered"!

Have you ever offered God a bartering prayer—an "If You do this, I'll do that" kind of plea? If so, write about it below:

Sheth lived in the home of a man whose name meant "bartered" because he was an orphan. Maybe you, too, know what it's like to feel orphaned because your parents are no longer here on earth. Maybe you have picked up the phone to call them and then remembered they're gone. Death leaves us behind, feeling alone.

Sometimes, even worse than the death of parents is alienation from parents who are still alive, leaving us feeling alone. Broken homes can leave us feeling alone. Addictions that manipulate the will of those we love can leave us feeling alone. Alzheimer's, which steals our loved ones' minds, can leave us feeling alone. But as we learned yesterday, God doesn't leave us alone in Lo-debar.

Mephibosheth's hurts were no fault of his own. Sometimes we, too, experience hurts that are not our fault. Often this makes our pain even harder because there's no one on earth to blame. So sometimes we blame God.

Maybe you have been diagnosed with cancer despite the fact that you've always eaten healthy, exercised, never smoked a day in your life, and routinely worn sunscreen. Maybe you have suffered verbal abuse from a person who was raised in a home where words hurt their heart. Many innocent children have been physically or sexually abused. Often, women who are victimized early in life choose abusive men.

Hurting people often hurt others. Maybe you were hurt on purpose, and your perpetrator knew exactly what they were doing. Maybe you were shortchanged or outright swindled. Maybe the offender needed to feed their children, or maybe they were simply greedy and preyed on you because of your benevolence.

Often, we feel shame when we're victimized, even though we did nothing to deserve it. Sometimes our hurts are so complex that we can't untangle the knots of what's been done to us. All we can do is lay the whole snarled mess of emotional barbed wire at the feet of our King and ask Him to heal our hearts, because living in fear of being hurt again is no way to live.

Mephibosheth surely feared being found and hurt by David. He likely lived for years looking over his shoulder, staying in the shadows, and trying to be invisible and small when in public. He may have begged Makir to keep his secret because he feared the knock on the door.

Fearing the dreaded knock on the door is hard. We each have experienced a knock we can't outrun at some point:

- the divorce documents formally delivered by an attorney,
- the unexpected layoff notice,
- a call from the school to say your child has been hurt, or

- the mechanic's explanation that the car you rely on for everything needs repairs you can't afford.

When a heart is breaking, friends need friends to be by their side—to carry them as they cry out to God. Even in the absence of friends, our King is always listening. Always present to comfort. Please know this: We never need to barter with God, because He wants to help us.

We never need to barter with God, because He wants to help us.

"Are you tired? Worn out? Burned out on religion? Come to me. Get away with me and you'll recover your life. I'll show you how to take a real rest. Walk with me and work with me—watch how I do it. Learn the unforced rhythms of grace. I won't lay anything heavy or ill-fitting on you. Keep company with me and you'll learn to live freely and lightly."

—Matthew 11:28-30 MSG

Read Matthew 11:28-30 in the margin. Where does this passage connect with your real life today?

Our King wants us to live "freely and lightly." Whatever our battle or burden might be, He wants to teach us "the unforced rhythms of grace." He wants to provide soul-satisfying rest. We don't need to barter with God because He wants us to come to Him to exchange our weariness for rest and our burdens for peace that passes understanding.

Look up 2 Corinthians 4:8-9. Then draw lines to match the pairs below.

We are pressed on every side by troubles,	but never abandoned by God.
We are perplexed,	but not driven to despair.
We are hunted down,	but we are not destroyed.
We get knocked down,	but we are not crushed.

I don't have all the answers for why bad things happen to good people; no one does. But I do know that during trials, I cling to Scripture like my little girl clung to the bottom bar of the grocery cart to keep from being run over. Paul reminds us that even when we feel pressed, perplexed, or knocked down, we are never crushed, abandoned, or destroyed. God holds us steady in every storm, giving us strength that outlasts the weight of whatever we're facing. And somehow, in His quiet way, He keeps lifting our hearts back into the light!

Reread this week's memory verse and fill in the blanks.

"Do not be __________ or discouraged, for the ________ will personally go ahead of you. He will be with you; he will neither__________ you nor abandon you."

—Deuteronomy 31:8

Enter into a time of worship. Scan this QR code to listen to "Living Hope" by Phil Wickham.

Write your name in the blank and let this become the blessing Jesus whispers over your heart.

Come to Me, beloved__________________. Do not wait for a better moment or a better version of yourself. I am your King, yet I draw you close with the tenderness of perfect love. You never need to barter with Me—your efforts, goodness, and strength are not the price of My presence. Simply bring your need and I will meet you with mercy, not measurement. My throne of grace overflows with help. Step boldly toward Me, confident that you are cherished. I delight when you trust My heart enough to come without hesitation. My arms are already open.

Now offer your response: *Jesus, . . .*

Day 5: Fearing Exposure

Biblical Foundations:
2 Samuel 9:5; Esther 4:14; Psalm 56:3-4; Isaiah 41:13; Mark 6:50b

Focus Scripture:
So David sent for him and brought him from Makir's home. —2 Samuel 9:5

Yesterday I shared the story of my cancer scare, which, thankfully, turned out to be fibrocystic breast disease. I also shared how I found myself bartering with God for my life so I could raise my children—much as Mephibosheth may have bartered for protection with Makir as he grew into adulthood, living hidden in his home. From the time Sheth could remember, he must have lived in fear of being found out, exposed.

I have a dear friend I've known since high school who lives with the crippling fear of being found out, exposed, in a different way, as I recently found out.

We were celebrating Jenny's birthday and, with tears in her eyes, she shared that she didn't feel worthy for me to buy her lunch. She explained that there isn't a day that she doesn't live with some degree of fear. Accomplished in her field and surrounded by a wonderful family, she nevertheless carries her father's voice like a shadow.

Years of following Jesus and countless hours of counseling haven't erased the fear that she'll wake up alone one day, convinced his words have finally been proven true.

"No man will ever want you."

"You're not that pretty or smart."

My heart breaks as I think of these crippling lies that have injected fear into Jenny's veins since she was the age of young Sheth. It has made her journey through life very hard. Mephibosheth entered hiding as a small child. Today we will learn that he did not come out of hiding until he was summoned.

Read 2 Samuel 9:5 in the margin. Who summoned Mephibosheth? How do you imagine he felt when receiving that summons?

So David sent for him and brought him from Makir's home.

—2 Samuel 9:5

Lo-debar was roughly seventy to eighty miles from Jerusalem. That distance must have felt even longer to a man who likely believed he was being summoned to his own execution. With every mile, fear would have pressed more heavily on his chest. Though still young, I imagine Sheth walked hunched over like an old man worn down by dread.

When Mephibosheth left Lo-debar behind, he would have descended dusty slopes toward the Jordan River. The valley below was hot, humid, and without bridges. He would have needed help to cross the rushing waters. Did he have someone to help him, or did he have to wait hours for a passerby to show him mercy? We will never know. On the far side of the river, the road climbed sharply into the Judean hills—narrow, twisting paths carved into rugged mountainsides.

The journey likely took at least a week or longer. That meant nights spent in open fields or crowded village courtyards, with dust for a pillow and fear for a blanket. Every jolt of the rocky road would have reminded him of his physical brokenness. Every sunrise would have brought him closer to the king whom his grandfather had tried to kill on multiple occasions. And with every step, the same question must have echoed in his mind: What will happen when I finally stand before the king?

Like Sheth, fear of being found out or exposed drives us into hiding, where loneliness becomes our dreaded companion. It is such a common occurrence in our world today that we have dubbed the feeling "impostor syndrome." As women, we commonly carry a quiet, persistent fear of being found out—a sense that beneath our calm exterior lies a collection of insecurities, doubts, and hidden struggles. This feeling isn't a flaw in character; it's a deeply human response to the pressure to appear capable, composed, and endlessly resilient.

At the heart of this fear lies a quiet belief: that others see us as more confident, qualified, or spiritually grounded than we truly feel. The distance between the outer image and the inner experience creates a steady hum of self-doubt. Social media, with its AI-polished pictures and curated perfection, only widens the gap. Beneath the glossy surface are hearts that feel fractured. In those hidden places, despair whispers in the shadows.

We move through our days projecting steadiness while privately wondering if we're doing enough or doing it well. This often blends with the pressure to balance multiple roles—caregiver, professional, friend, ministry leader, partner—while fearing that someone might notice the exhaustion or feelings of being overwhelmed beneath the surface. Even normal human limits can feel like personal shortcomings when the world expects strength without pause. I have felt this strain often.

[Fear of being found out] is such a common occurrence in our world today that we have dubbed the feeling "imposter syndrome."

When have you felt that you weren't doing enough—or doing something well enough? What did you believe about yourself in that moment?

Spiritual life adds another layer. We often fear being exposed as less mature, less consistent, or less faithful than others believe we are. Doubts, dry seasons, or unanswered questions can feel like secrets that must be hidden to maintain the appearance of spiritual steadiness. Emotional struggles—anxiety, sadness, insecurity—are tucked away behind practiced smiles.

There is also the fear of not living up to our reputation. Past mistakes, messy relationships, or private battles can feel like shadows that could be revealed. Even the simple chaos of daily life—disorganized spaces, forgotten tasks, unfinished projects, or cranky kids—can spark the worry that others would judge us if they saw the unfiltered version.

As you reflect on the fear of being "found out," which of these descriptions echoes your own experience? Check as many as apply.

___ Feeling less confident or capable than others assume

___ Struggling to balance everything and fearing someone will notice

___ Hiding exhaustion or feelings of being emotionally overwhelmed behind a smile

___ Worrying you're not as spiritually mature as people think

___ Worrying you're not as smart as people think

___ Carrying past mistakes or messy relationships you hope will remain hidden

___ Feeling disorganized or chaotic beneath a polished exterior

___ Fearing you're not truly liked or accepted

___ Other: ____

Naming these fears is the first step. When we realize how common these feelings are, the pressure eases. The fear of being "found out" loses its power when brought into the light, where compassion, connection, and truth can replace the quiet burden of pretending. This shared honesty becomes a doorway to freedom—an invitation to rest in the truth that we are already loved, valued, and enough.

Even more transformative is turning to God's Word for truth that displaces fear and lies. "Do not fear" is the most repeated command in Scripture—not because God expects us to muster courage on our own, but because He continuously reveals His steadfast presence. From Genesis to Revelation, this invitation flows from God's character, not from our capability.

Fear begins to lose its grip when we remember who goes before us: the Creator who brings order from chaos, the Redeemer who enters our suffering, and the Shepherd who leads us through the valley. Scripture never promises a life without threats, but it does promise a God who is greater than every threat. To obey "Do not fear" is to shift our gaze from what unsettles us to the One who upholds us with His righteous hand.

"Do not fear" is the most repeated command in Scripture.

Which of these verses most resonates with your heart today? Put a check mark beside it.

"For I hold you by your right hand—
I, the Lord your God.
And I say to you,
'Don't be afraid. I am here to help you.' "
—Isaiah 41:13

But when I am afraid,
I will put my trust in you.
I praise God for what he has promised.
I trust in God, so why should I be afraid?
What can mere mortals do to me?
—Psalm 56:3-4

Jesus spoke to them at once. "Don't be afraid,"
he said. "Take courage! I am here!"
—Mark 6:50b

Now write each scripture reference on the shield below.

Fear begins to lose its power when we lift God's truth as our shield.

As we close this week, I want to leave you with a story. If you've ever watched *The Bachelor*, you might notice a few similarities between the show and a young woman in the Bible named Esther.

Esther was one of many beautiful young women brought to the palace when King Xerxes was looking for a new queen, and she won his heart and the crown. However, she lived with the constant tension of hiding her identity as a Jew in a foreign court, as advised by her uncle Mordecai. That tension would become a turning point when a decree of annihilation was issued against the Jews, and Mordecai asked Esther to go into the king's presence and plead for her people. Like Sheth, she was likely a young adult when she was called to face fears far bigger than herself.

Look up Esther 4:11-14. What was Esther's concern about doing what Mordecai requested?

What was Mordecai's response? ______________________________

If you remain silent, then ______________________________

Who knows if ______________________________

If we read the rest of Esther's story, we see that she discovered she had indeed been placed in the kingdom *for such a time as this*. Esther chose courage over self-protection, risking her life by approaching the king uninvited to speak boldly on behalf of her people, becoming an instrument of God's deliverance.

Esther is one of only two women in Scripture—alongside Ruth—to have a book named after her, and hers is the only one in which God's name is never mentioned. Still, His fingerprints cover every scene: guiding her steps, turning the king's heart, exposing evil, and lifting an ordinary young woman into extraordinary courage.

Esther's story reveals a God who works in the backstory, arranging freedom long before His people know they need it. With that same God beside us, we, too, can be free from fear and rise like Esther—to stand, to speak, and to intercede for our families, our communities, and our nation. May this week's truth settle deep within you: Fear doesn't get the final word when God is writing the story!

Reread this week's memory verse and fill in the blanks.

"Do not be______________ or discouraged, for the ___________________ will personally go ahead of you. He will be with you; he will neither______________ you nor abandon you."

—Deuteronomy 31:8

Enter into a time of worship. Scan this QR code to listen to "Fear Is a Liar" by Zach Williams.

Write your name in the blank and let this become the blessing Jesus whispers over your heart.

My beloved________________, come to Me and rest. I see the weight you hide behind your smile and the swirl of responsibilities that leave you weary. I know the doubts that whisper "you're not enough." Do not fear, for I go before you and walk beside you. Nothing in your past or present can separate you from My delight. Let My presence quiet your striving and steady your breath. You are enough because I am with you, and I will not abandon you.

Now offer your response: *Jesus, . . .*

Week 2

Video Viewer Guide

1. Shame is focused on the person. Guilt is focused on the ____________.

2. Shame is debilitating. Guilt is ____________ when we turn to God.

3. Shame says I did something bad, therefore, I am bad. Guilt says the ____________ is bad.

4. Shame says you are unforgivable. Guilt says return to God for ____________.

5. Sometimes it's not the ____________ battle that breaks us; it's the ____________ thing that comes after the big battle, when we're already drained.

6. Even the most faithful servants of God experience ____________.

7. ____________, when mixed with ____________, often turns into despair.

8. God ministers to Elijah's physical needs ____________ addressing his emotional and spiritual ones, a powerful reminder that our ____________ matter.

9. Ministering to others doesn't always look like preaching or teaching. Sometimes it looks like nourishing ____________ and ____________.

10. Seeking help is not a lack of ____________. It is ____________.

WEEK 3

Being Invited to the Table

Memory Verse

So let us come boldly to the throne of our gracious God. There we will receive his mercy, and we will find grace to help us when we need it most.

—Hebrews 4:16

Recipe of the Week

Our recipe this week is for Scrumptious Granola. My hope is that someone will volunteer to prepare the recipe, and it might sweeten your time together in fellowship.

Introduction to This Week

2 Samuel 9:6-13

This week brings us to the turning point in Mephibosheth's life. In the first two weeks of our study, we saw that Mephibosheth's childhood was marked by tragedy—dropped, crippled, and hidden away. But this week, we watch him step into a new world on the brink of transformation and restoration. You'll be encouraged as you see his inheritance restored and witness him receive an invitation of a lifetime to dine at the king's table.

What makes this invitation so life-changing is simple: Sheth took the king at his word. He did nothing to earn the king's favor or the invitation; it was given by grace. In the same way, we do nothing to earn our King's favor or invitation; it is given by grace. He wants to restore us and renew us. This week is a journey of accepting His love and being changed by His presence.

Day 1: Come to the King

Biblical Foundations:
1 Samuel 1:2, 10-11; 2 Samuel 9:6a-b; Hebrews 4:16

Focus Scripture:
His name was Mephibosheth; he was Jonathan's son and Saul's grandson. When he came to David, he bowed low to the ground in deep respect.

—2 Samuel 9:6a-b

I'm so excited about this week! Let's jump right in with both feet. When Mephibosheth bowed before King David, he likely braced for death. Though his feet carried him into the throne room, every step came with struggle—a limp that told the story of his past. And here we are, arriving with feet that move freely—often without thinking, often without noticing. The very thing Sheth lacked physically is what we often take for granted spiritually: the ability to come freely, boldly, and confidently before our King.

Reread today's Focus Scripture, 2 Samuel 9:6a-b (above). How would you describe Mephibosheth's bow?

This was no ordinary bow. It was the bow of a lifetime—the bow that Sheth surely had dreaded, fearing he might lose his head. This wasn't a slight bend at the waist or an obligatory head nod. I'm convinced this was a fall-to-your-knees, face-to-the-floor, spare-my-life kind of bow—a posture of complete surrender. Though he was disabled, we're told that Sheth bowed low.

Imagine how difficult it must have been for Sheth to lower himself to the ground and then struggle back to his feet. His movements were likely uncoordinated, cumbersome, and even awkward to watch. Yet he bowed low anyway. In that trembling bow, unfathomable mercy met him—mercy that outran his limp and overcame his shame. He bowed in brokenness, and the king lifted him in kindness.

Because our study is in 2 Samuel, it's the perfect moment to remember another bow of sorts—one offered in prayer by Samuel's mother, Hannah. Just as Sheth bowed low before King David in desperate submission, Hannah bowed low before the King of kings in desperate prayer. If you've ever carried a prayer so deep it felt like it lived in your bones, you'll find a kindred spirit in Hannah. Her prayerful surrender teaches us what it means to bring our whole selves before God.

Read 1 Samuel 1:2. What do we learn about Hannah in this verse?

The last sentence of this verse holds such pain. In Hannah's culture, sharing a husband was accepted although never endorsed by God. Motherhood was considered a woman's crowning glory, and Hannah's empty arms felt like a public billboard announcing her private pain. To make matters worse, Peninnah would taunt Hannah year after year, especially during the family's annual trip to worship at the temple in Shiloh. Imagine trying to worship while someone pokes your deepest wound.

Although Hannah was *sorrowful,* she remained *steadfast.* She carried her ache straight to God. One year, after the sacrificial meal, she slipped away to the tabernacle. There, she poured out her heart in a prayer so raw and earnest that the priest, Eli, assumed she was drunk—proof that passionate prayer can look a little messy, much like Sheth's awkward low bow before David. When she explained her anguish, Eli blessed her and assured her that God would grant her request. Before leaving, Hannah made a vow.

Now read 1 Samuel 1:10-11. What did Hannah promise God if He would give her a son?

If God granted her a son, Hannah was offering her future child under the Nazirite vow—a life visibly set apart by abstaining from wine, avoiding ritual impurity, and never cutting one's hair. So when Hannah said that "his hair will never be cut" (1 Samuel 1:11), she was dedicating her hoped-for son to lifelong service. It was a mother's vow of total release, trusting God with the child she longed for more than anything.

Just as David would remember Sheth, in one of Scripture's most tender turnarounds, so God had remembered Hannah. She conceived and bore a son, naming him Samuel, which means "heard of God."[1] When Samuel was weaned, she brought him to Eli at the tabernacle. It's one of the most bittersweet scenes in the Old Testament: a mother offering her only son. In this way Samuel was an Old Testament foreshadowing of Christ. Yet Hannah wasn't giving Samuel *up*; she was giving him *back*. Her surrender was worship, not loss.

Can you recall a time when you sensed God inviting you to return something precious to Him? If so, describe it below:

Samuel grew into one of Israel's greatest prophets—the one who anointed both Saul and David, whose lives would later shape Mephibosheth's story. Years after Hannah approached God humbly in prayer, we watch Mephibosheth approach King David with humility. Hannah and Sheth's stories echo each other: two souls carrying sorrow, two hearts learning to trust.

Both Hannah and Mephibosheth remind us that when we come before our King—fragile, honest, and unguarded—He meets us there. Not with distance, but with compassion. Not with dismissal, but with care. In our barrenness, our King welcomes us and listens.

We face seasons marked by many kinds of barrenness.

Check all the statements that describe the ways "barrenness" shows up in your life, completing this sentence: I . . .

___ am always tired.

___ feel invisible.

___ lose myself in responsibilities.

___ sometimes feel disconnected from friends.

___ live in survival mode.

___ am stuck in routines.

___ feel emotionally numb.

___ feel like my efforts don't matter.

___ have unhealed grief.

___ have dreams deferred.

___ experience relational loneliness.

___ feel spiritually dry.

We can learn from both Hannah and Sheth to bring the empty places within us to the feet of our King and bow low in prayer. There, in His presence, our disappointments become holy surrender, our fears become trust restored, and our pain becomes a place of meeting with our King—where we are broken yet beloved. You can trust His invitation to come to Him. When you bow low, He will lift you high, holding you secure in His love. By surrendering your heart, you will discover freedom from fear.

Sheth found mercy when He responded to King David's invitation and bowed before him. And we are extended a similar invitation. This royal invitation is deeply moving when we understand that ancient kings positioned soldiers wielding massive blades to guard the doors of their throne room, ready to strike down anyone who approached uninvited.

So let us come boldly to the throne of our gracious God. There we will receive his mercy, and we will find grace to help us when we need it most.
—*Hebrews 4:16*

Read Hebrews 4:16 in the margin. How are we to come before God's throne?

Label the swords of the guardsmen with the two things we will receive from our gracious God.

For imperfect people like Mephibosheth, throne rooms generally were places of fear, not welcome. Yet God invites us to *come boldly*, without trembling or fear of rejection. Instead of punishment, we find mercy and grace poured out exactly when we need refuge and love.

For this reason, Hebrews 4:16 will serve as our memory verse for this triumphant week. As you meditate on these beautiful words throughout the week, may courage rise in you to approach God just as you are, confident that mercy and grace await you there.

Enter into a time of worship. Scan this QR code to listen to "O Come to the Altar" by Elevation Worship.

Reread this week's memory verse once more:

So let us come boldly to the throne of our gracious God. There we will receive his mercy, and we will find grace to help us when we need it most.
—Hebrews 4:16

What stands out to you in this verse?

Write your name in the blank and let this become the blessing Jesus whispers over your heart.

My beloved_________________, come boldly before My throne and bring the barrenness you carry—your disappointments, fears, unanswered longings, and the quiet ache of feeling overlooked or forgotten. Lay them at My feet. Nothing you surrender is wasted in My hands. I am the One who fills empty places, restores what feels lost, and breathes life where hope has thinned. Rest in My presence. Let My love steady your trembling heart and soften the places you've guarded for too long. When you bow low, I will lift you high, just as I lifted Hannah and Sheth.

Now offer your response: *Jesus, . . .*

Day 2: You Are Enough

Biblical Foundations:
2 Samuel 9:6c-d; Mark 6:31; John 6:8-9, 13; 2 Corinthians 1:3-4

Focus Scripture:
David said, "Greetings, Mephibosheth." Mephibosheth replied, "I am your servant."
—2 Samuel 9:6c-d

Yesterday we watched Mephibosheth bow before King David for the first time. When he rose, he was still breathing. David hadn't beheaded him. Years of fear must have poured out in one long, trembling exhale as he tried to process the shock of being spared. I imagine Sheth thinking, *If David isn't going to kill me, why am I here?*

Once the overwhelming fear of losing his head subsided, Mephibosheth likely felt deeply out of place. He hadn't seen a palace in his entire adult life. In biblical times, people with disabilities weren't welcomed into such spaces. Sheth is one of the few disabled people in Scripture ever given a royal invitation. Standing before David, Sheth must have felt small and "not enough." Perhaps he had felt that way from the time he was five, and his nurse dropped him, crippling him in both feet.

I remember being five and heading into first grade with crooked bangs, cut by my mom, and a timid smile—all captured by my school picture. Then in second grade, the very month I finally got my new front tooth, I tripped on our uneven brick patio and broke it. From that moment on, I was known as the girl with the chipped front tooth. I was self-conscious and didn't feel pretty. I tried to hide my teeth by not smiling.

In high school, I was ostracized for my faith. I tried to counterbalance my insecurities by becoming a good student, but even that didn't come easily. I was awkward, unsure, and average in every class but English.

What were some of your insecurities when you were growing up?

When I left my farming community to study pharmacy in college, I was convinced I wasn't smart enough. My first pharmacy calculations exam seemed to prove it. I scored a 57 percent—not because I couldn't convert drams to ounces to milligrams, but because I couldn't remember my times tables. Calculators were forbidden.

I stood in the dorm hallway at the communal phone, trying not to cry as I shared with my folks that I had failed an exam. Dad was working long hours to help with tuition. Grandma had proudly told everyone I was becoming a "farmist." I couldn't flunk out.

By the grace of God, I made it through those grueling years and moved to Kansas City for my first job. Community pharmacists must be fast and accurate. I could manage one or the other, but not both. Patients stacked up at the pick-up window checking their watches as if to say, "How hard is counting thirty pills?"

What they didn't know was that I couldn't read most of their prescriptions. I had mastered chemical equations and molecular structures, but no one had taught us how to decipher physicians' handwriting. My heart raced every time I held an illegible script, knowing that a thousand drugs were behind me and that choosing the wrong one could harm someone. Looking back, I realize I was suffering from daily anxiety, yet somehow I was promoted to pharmacy manager. I kept striving, desperate to be enough.

Around that time, I married Dave, who was worn thin from his own long hours. Then I became a mom with no one to help me—my own mother was two states away. My daughter cried inconsolably her entire first year, and I felt like I was failing her too.

I was in my twenties—about the age of Mephibosheth in today's reading—and drowning in the "not enoughs."

When and how have you felt you were not enough?

One day during this difficult season, God met me in the most ordinary yet spectacular way as I was studying Scripture. Though not audible, I felt He spoke to me through a familiar miracle: the feeding of the five thousand. Before that day, I'd read the story countless times and had dismissed it as a miracle about food. But on that day, Jesus opened my eyes, and the first thing He showed me was His own weariness.

Read Mark 6:31 in the margin. Why was Jesus tired, and what was He planning to do?

Then Jesus said, "Let's go off by ourselves to a quiet place and rest awhile." He said this because there were so many people coming and going that Jesus and his apostles didn't even have time to eat.

—Mark 6:31

As women, we know that feeling—so many people to care for that we don't even stop or sit down to eat. As a full-time pharmacist, wife, and mom, I was familiar with exhaustion. I was worn and weary.

Read John 6:9 in the margin for more details. Who provided the barley loaves and fishes?

"There's a young boy here with five barley loaves and two fish. But what good is that with this huge crowd?"

—John 6:9

That day, as I reread the familiar miracle, I—like the young boy with a small lunch—could offer only what I had: five crumby croutons and two goldfish crackers' worth of worn-thin hope and stamina. But I gave it anyway. Jesus took what was small, ordinary, and insufficient and blessed it. Then, offering it to His Father, He broke it. And as He did, something in me broke too. I sobbed, feeling fragile yet deeply held; broken, yet beloved in the arms of my King.

Through tears, I read in my study Bible notes that the five loaves were biscuit-sized and made from barley, the grain used to feed livestock and the poor. The two fish were tiny—probably the size of sardines—meant as condiments, not protein sources.[2]

I sensed Jesus asking me, "Lisa, who do you think packed that young boy's lunch?" I knew instantly; it was his momma. And I wept again, because I imagined her wishing she had more than barley to use in her bread. I carried my own mom guilt from exhaustion and impatience. She likely carried hers from poverty. Yet barley in Jesus's hands was enough. Five loaves and two fish fed thousands.

In that society, women and children weren't counted, but Jesus counted them and used them to minister to others. And in that moment, I knew He counted me too. I felt Him cradle my weary heart, soothing my sobs and telling me I was enough.

That moment became a turning point for me, just as coming before David was a turning point for Sheth. For the first time since becoming a pharmacist, a wife, and a mother, I knew that with Jesus, I could and would be enough.

Just as Mephibosheth likely felt he was less than enough, many of us carry a similar ache, pressed by expectations around caregiving, career, and beauty. Yet the same Jesus who counted the uncounted whispers worth and dignity over us today.

Reread today's Focus Scripture, 2 Samuel 9:6c-d (page 91). Picture yourself standing with King David and Sheth in that moment. What tone do you imagine in David's voice? How might that tone lift Sheth's eyes? Write your thoughts below.

David wasn't merely addressing a subject; he was welcoming a person who had long lived in the shadows of fear and unworthiness. King David received Mephibosheth without hesitation, without conditions, without asking him to prove anything. He affirmed Sheth as he was. Likewise, even when we feel small, inadequate, or painfully aware of our limitations—whether in our service, our relationships, or our inner life—our King meets us with that same steady welcome. We are not measured by our perfection but held by a love that does not waver.

We are more than enough, not because we have earned it, but because our King's love and acceptance are more than enough. And when that truth sinks in, it has the power to lift our gaze, soften our fears, and remind us that our presence in God's story is intentional, cherished, and secure.

Reread this week's memory verse and fill in the blank.

So let us come ____________ to the throne of our gracious God. There we will receive his mercy, and we will find grace to help us when we need it most.

—Hebrews 4:16

Write your name in the blank and let this become the blessing Jesus whispers over your heart.

Come to Me, ______________, with whatever you carry. Bring your hopes, your weariness, and the pieces you're not sure matter. Place them in My hands. I lift what you offer to the Father, bless it, and break it so that it can be shared. What seems insufficient to you becomes more than enough in Me. I will use your surrendered offering to accomplish My will and meet the needs of those I've called you to serve. Do not fear the size of your gift. Trust the power of My touch and let Me multiply what you release.

Now offer your response: *Jesus, . . .*

Enter into a time of worship. Scan this QR code to listen to "Run To the Father" by Cody Carnes.

Day 3: You Can Trust the King

Biblical Foundations:
2 Samuel 9:7a; Psalm 46:1-2; Jeremiah 29:11

Focus Scripture:
"Don't be afraid!" David said. "I intend to show kindness to you because of my promise to your father, Jonathan." —2 Samuel 9:7a

I have a grandson who's almost five—Mephibosheth's age when we first met him. He plays hard. He runs and jumps and then hoots and hollers with all the joy and abandon little boys carry. I imagine Mephibosheth did all the rough-and-tumble things boys do until that frightful day when his father died, and his nanny dropped him.

Because Jonathan and David were close friends, it's likely that David met Sheth, and it's possible that Sheth had memories of David. Or, like most preschoolers, perhaps he didn't pay much attention to his father's friends. In any case, it's understandable why Sheth would have doubted he could trust the new king of Israel, who replaced his grandfather, since former royal heirs were rarely shown mercy.

In the face of disappointments and tragedy, have you ever wondered if you could trust God? If so, what made trusting God difficult?

Most of us struggle with questions and doubts when life breaks us in painful ways. I believe one of the reasons God wants us to know Sheth's story is to help us see His unwavering trustworthiness. Just as David faithfully honored his promise to Jonathan out of deep love, our King of kings keeps His promises to us with a love even greater.

Scripture is overflowing with the promises of God. Many theologians place the number of divine promises *in the thousands*—between three and eight thousand, depending on how they are categorized. That's a lot of promises! The message is clear: Our King is a Promise Keeper, and His love toward us is steadfast. Perhaps we question God's perfect faithfulness because we know ourselves—and others—are not perfectly faithful. But God is not like us. His character does not shift. His love does not waver. His promises do not expire.

My childhood friend Cathy knows firsthand what unfaithfulness feels like. Perhaps you can relate to her story in some way. Her husband struggled with addiction. When he was sober, he was faithful. They made a life together and enjoyed many lovely moments with their five sons. But when he was drunk, he was unfaithful. Anyone who has loved an addict knows the pain of broken promises.

As the drinking episodes became more frequent and his business began to fail, she prayed harder for his healing. Then late one night, the phone call came. He had died in a car crash. Her heart was crushed—both by the loss of her husband and by the damage his addiction had caused their family. After struggling financially to raise their five children alone for almost a decade, Cathy met another faith-filled man who did not suffer from addiction. They shared so many qualities in common. Best of all, he had a heart for Jesus and a heart for Cathy. He asked her to be his bride.

Their wedding was a beautiful covenant of love. The first several months were wonderful, until distrust began to creep back into Cathy's heart. If he called home saying he would be late from work, she panicked, thinking the worst. She questioned his faithfulness and began to track him on his phone. Then she began to track him in her car. Fear woke Cathy up at night. Though her husband slept right next to her, she felt abandoned, like she had felt when her first husband would disappear for days at a time.

If you have experienced unfaithfulness, you understand how difficult it is to trust again. You understand how fear strangles trust. Children who have been abandoned by a parent often have issues trusting as well. If you've been burned by a business partner, pastor, neighbor, or friend, trusting another may prove difficult. Fear may wake you up at night as it woke Cathy—and as it likely woke Sheth. Like Cathy, you can also find support through counseling at your church. As she continues her journey, the moments when fear rises are now met with a growing steadiness. She's learning that healing unfolds over time as she places her hope in a God who has proven Himself trustworthy.

God is our refuge and strength,
always ready to help in times of trouble.
So we will not fear when earthquakes come
and the mountains crumble into the sea.
—*Psalm 46:1-2*

Read Psalm 46:1-2 in the margin. Label the "mountains" of fear in your life that, with God's help, could crumble.

Reread our Focus Scripture for today, 2 Samuel 9:7a (page 96). How did David respond to Mephibosheth's fear?

David likely saw Mephibosheth's fear. Sheth likely kept his eyes fixed on the feet of the one who held his fate in his hands. Wanting to comfort him, David spoke these three words immediately after greeting him: "Don't be afraid!"

Throughout Scripture, God repeatedly speaks the same steadying command: "Do not be afraid." (See, for example, Isaiah 41:10; Joshua 1:9; and Luke 1:30.) It appears more often than any other instruction—not because fear is unusual, but because God knows how quickly our hearts tremble. Scripture repeats variations of "Do not fear" more than seventy times directly—and offers hundreds more related encouragements. But despite the common claim that there's one for every day of the year, the count is not a neat 365.

From Abraham's reassurance from the Lord (Genesis 15:1) to the angel's words to the women at the empty tomb (Matthew 28:5), God meets His people in uncertainty and anchors them with His presence. Fear fades when confronted by the character of the King who stands with us.

Read Jeremiah 29:11 in the margin. Imagine living with the certainty of this promise. How might it change the way you respond to trials, setbacks, or fears?

"For I know the plans I have for you," says the LORD. "They are plans for good and not for disaster, to give you a future and a hope."

—Jeremiah 29:11

Mephibosheth could trust King David, just as we can trust our King of kings. And just as David extended a future and a hope to Sheth, *Jesus invites us to step into the life He has promised*—a life marked by peace, courage, and hope that no brokenness or challenge can take away. In the coming days, we will see more clearly how David gave Sheth a future and a hope—and we will be reminded that the same King who cared for him cares for us.

As you conclude your time of study today, ask yourself this question: *Will I let Jesus's peace guard my heart and mind, even when fear and uncertainty come?*

Reread this week's memory verse and fill in the blanks.

So let us come __________ *to the throne of our gracious God. There we will receive his* __________*, and we will find grace to help us when we need it most.*

—Hebrews 4:16

Enter into a time of worship. Scan this QR code to listen to "Been So Good" by Elevation Worship.

Write your name in the blank and let this become the blessing Jesus whispers over your heart.

My beloved ________________ , do not fear. Come boldly before My throne whenever you need grace or mercy; I will never turn you away. I hold your future in My hands—one filled with goodness, purpose, and hope. Let Me gift you the peace of mind and heart the world cannot give, a peace that settles you from the inside out. I am strengthening you even now, lifting the weight you were never meant to carry. Rest in Me. Trust My timing, My heart, My faithfulness. I am your refuge, your steady place, your trustworthy God, and I delight in caring for you.

Now offer your response: *Jesus, . . .*

Day 4: You Are Accepted

Biblical Foundations:
2 Samuel 9:8; Hebrews 13:5; Revelation 19:5-8

Focus Scripture:
Mephibosheth bowed respectfully and exclaimed, "Who is your servant, that you should show such kindness to a dead dog like me?" —2 Samuel 9:8

He proposed, and she accepted. Time stood still in that perfect instant—as if the world itself paused to witness the first heartbeat of their forever. Their wedding day unfolded like a dream. Mary was radiant, and Mike looked dashing, his eyes shimmering with tears as he watched his beautiful bride glide toward him. After her father gently placed her hand in Mike's, together they spoke vows so tender that they moved the entire congregation to tears.

The reception overflowed with laughter, warmth, and joy. The same faith that had drawn them together—he, a youth pastor; she, a music director—inspired everyone who gathered to celebrate them. With a bubble send-off after the reception, they stepped into their future, tiny spheres of hope floating around them like whispered promises.

In the years that followed, they welcomed three beautiful children. Mike stepped confidently into his role as lead pastor of a thriving church, while Mary poured her whole heart into nurturing their family. Between cheering from bleachers and supporting her teens through every team they joined, she began to notice something unsettling. In the mornings, her hands and feet throbbed with a swelling she could no longer blame on last night's salty dinner. Fatigue clung to her like a heavy coat she couldn't shrug off.

Eventually, she forced herself to make time for a doctor's visit. After rounds of exams, bloodwork, and imaging, she was sent to a rheumatologist. The diagnosis was rheumatoid arthritis, a progressive disease. Painful flare-ups. No cure. Still, she clung fiercely to gratitude for her family and their health, trusting Jesus through every shifting season, even as she sensed Mike drifting further away, unwilling to acknowledge her health struggles.

Then came the day her world quietly fractured.

She was standing at the kitchen table, struggling to fold a warm heap of laundry fresh from the dryer, her fingers stiff and aching. Mike walked in earlier than usual, before the children were home. He didn't sit. He didn't ease into conversation. Right there, in the center of their kitchen, he confessed he loved another woman.

Seventeen years of marriage burst like the fragile bubbles that had once floated around them as they left their wedding reception. Mary slipped into a deep and silent grief. Rejected, she felt frozen in fear—uncertain how to face a future she had never imagined.

You may not have experienced this exact scenario, but what causes you to fear? Fear is a four-letter word that forges forward fast when we feel alone. I've heard it said that there are two ways to react to fear, and the acronym F.E.A.R. spells out both options:

Forget **E**verything **A**nd **R**un
or
Face **E**verything **A**nd **R**ise[3]

So how do we, like Mary, rise above the fear of rejection so we can keep breathing when life hurts? We begin by recognizing that fear is a feeling. It's a normal response when we face the unknown, especially when we face the unknown alone. Mary felt frozen in fear. Sheth did too. And in our own ways, so have we.

Like Sheth, when have you fled in fear when facing an unwanted uncertainty—whether it was the uncertainty of a broken home, broken dreams, broken health, or something else?

Reread today's Focus Scripture, 2 Samuel 9:8 (page 101). How did Sheth bow before the king this second time?

Write in the blank on the left of this continuum line the name Sheth called himself. (You will complete the other side later in the lesson.)

This self-appointed name tells us that Sheth probably carried the weight of rejection, abandonment, and vulnerability. Like Mary, fear of rejection is a common fear many of us carry. It's often rooted in experiences that taught us to question our worth or brace for disappointment. Early wounds, past betrayals, or seasons of feeling unseen can leave our hearts tender, making connection feel risky.

Cultural expectations add pressure to be pleasing, perfect, or endlessly available, and when we fall short of those impossible standards, it's easy to assume rejection is waiting around the corner. Even our own inner critic can become a voice that reinforces old fears. Yet beneath this reality is a deeper and more powerful truth: Fear of rejection grows in the shadows, but it loosens its grip in the light of compassion, belonging, and grace.

As a community of women, we can share our stories, challenge the lies that shaped them, and rest in the steady love of God and the support of trusted people around us. As we do this, something beautiful returns. The heart remembers it was made for connection, not isolation.

Fear may still whisper, but it no longer gets the final word. Hope does. And hope gently invites each of us to step forward—not because we are certain we will be accepted by others, but because we are learning we are already loved by our King.

> "Never will I leave you;
> never will I forsake you."
> —***Hebrews 13:5 NIV***

Read Hebrews 13:5 in the margin and circle the word *never*.

Sheth lost his father, and Mary lost her husband, but we have a Bridegroom who will *never* leave us or forsake us for another.

Look up Revelation 19:5-8. According to these verses, why are we to rejoice and be glad?

Verse 7 and 8 remind us that *we* are the beautiful *bride* of Christ—given the finest pure white linen to wear.

Write *bride* in the blank on the right side of the continuum on page 103, opposite the name *dead dog*.

Mary was left reeling after her husband left, but her story didn't end in that moment of heartbreak. She watched her husband's affair unravel, costing Mike both his credibility and his ministry. Through counseling, prayer, and a deepening faith, she slowly began to heal from the wounds of divorce and build a new life filled with purpose, meaning, and joy.

She saw restoration take shape in her children's lives as well, watching them grow, find remarkable spouses, and build families rooted in love. Hope began to take root again. Her journey didn't unfold the way she once imagined, yet gratitude now fills the places where sorrow lived. She knows God carried her through what once seemed too broken to ever be beautiful again. And she learned this truth firsthand: No brokenness is beyond redemption, and no heart is ever beyond the reach of God's enduring love.

Where in your own story might God be inviting you to trust that He can redeem what feels broken, just as He did for Mary?

Looking back, Mary can see God's mercy and grace woven through her story—mercy that she is *not* bound to someone who would resent her brokenness, and grace in living more abundantly and joyfully than she ever thought possible, despite her illness.

Sheth's story echoes the same pattern of mercy and grace. The first time he bowed before King David, he received mercy: his life was spared. The second time he bowed before the king, he received grace: a place at the king's table, an honor he never could have earned! Mary's life and Sheth's life preach the same truth:

Mercy	**Grace**
Mercy is not getting what we deserve.	Grace is getting what we could never deserve.
Mercy closes the door on punishment	Grace opens the door to on blessing.
Mercy erases the wrong.	Grace writes a new story.
Mercy spares us.	Grace supplies us.

And the best news of all: Our King offers us both with open hands!

Reread this week's memory verse and fill in the blank:

So let us come ________ *to the throne of our gracious God.*

There we will receive his ________, *and we will find* ________

to help us when we need it most.

—Hebrews 4:16

Enter into a time of worship. Scan this QR code to listen to "The Blessing" by Kari Jobe.

Write your name in the blank and let this become the blessing Jesus whispers over your heart.

My beloved ________________, *hear My voice. You are accepted. I call you My bride, My cherished one, My delight. I will never leave you or forsake you, even if others fail you. Lift your eyes, for I am preparing a place for you, and My heart is set on the great marriage feast where we will rejoice together forever.*

Now offer your response: *Jesus, . . .*

Day 5: You Are Restored

Biblical Foundations:
Ruth 1:16; 3:7-9, 11; 2 Samuel 9:9-10

Focus Scripture:
Then the king summoned Saul's servant Ziba and said, "I have given your master's grandson everything that belonged to Saul and his family. You and your sons and servants are to farm the land for him to produce food for your master's household. But Mephibosheth, your master's grandson, will eat here at my table." (Ziba had fifteen sons and twenty servants.) —2 Samuel 9:9-10

Yesterday I shared Mary's story—how she went from rejected to accepted as she was. Her journey reminds me of another woman in Scripture, one whose path feels just as tender and surprising. Her name is Ruth. Like Mary, Ruth's story began in the ache of loss. After her husband died, she clung to her grieving mother-in-law, Naomi, with a vow, which is commonly read today at weddings, stirring hearts with its beauty.

Look up Ruth 1:16. Then insert the missing words below into the crossword puzzle as directed:

"Don't ask me to (1 Across) you and turn back. Wherever you go, (2 Across); wherever you live, I will live. Your (1 Down) will be my (2 Down), and your (3 Across) will be my (3 Down)."

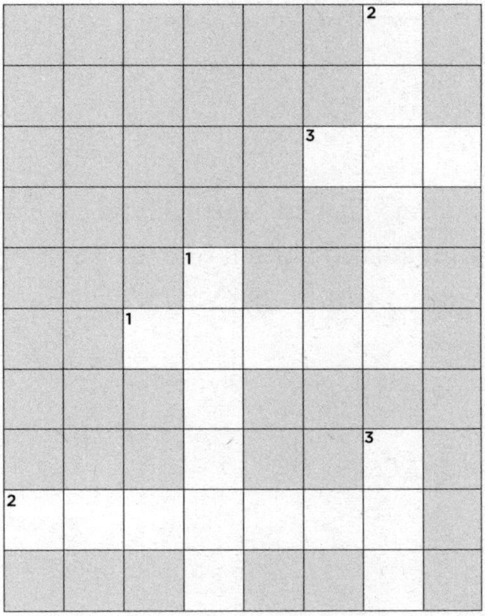

Similar to Mephibosheth's story, Ruth and Naomi started their journey impoverished, with nothing but broken dreams. Two widows with empty hands journeyed from Moab back to Bethlehem, carrying sorrow and a quiet hope that God might still write beauty into their story. To provide for them, Ruth headed out to glean in the fields, gathering leftover grain behind the harvesters. By divine design, she happened to wander into the field of Boaz—a man of standing, steady character, and quiet strength. Boaz noticed her courage, loyalty, and gentle spirit. He blessed her, protected her, and even invited her to share a meal with his workers (see Ruth 2:8-14).

It seems that something soft was beginning to kindle in Boaz—first respect, then affection; the kind that grew slow and steady like a warm ember. Naomi sensed God's hand in this and guided Ruth toward Boaz, her kinsman redeemer (a close male relative who steps in to rescue or restore a family member in need). Then came a tender moment on the threshing floor. After the harvest feast, Ruth approached quietly, finding Boaz asleep near the grain he was guarding. She lay at his feet—a humble, courageous request for covering, covenant, and a future only God could orchestrate. If you're like me and you're warmed by a good romance, you'll find this passage better than any Jane Austen novel.

Read Ruth 3:7-9. What stands out to you from these verses? How do they speak to your heart?

Boaz awakened, startled, and then he softened. This brave, virtuous woman had chosen him. In the glow of the fire, he spoke words every weary heart longs to hear.

"Do not fear. I will do for you all that you ask."

—Ruth 3:11 ESV

Read Ruth 3:11 in the margin. How do you imagine Ruth must have felt upon hearing these words?

It was a moment of holy romance—honor, protection, and promise wrapped in warmth and flickering light. Boaz redeemed Ruth, married her, and restored her mother-in-law Naomi's joy. Their son Obed became the grandfather of King David, placing Ruth—once a forlorn, foreign widow—into the very lineage of Christ (Matthew 1:5).

The role of a kinsman redeemer had been God's built-in provision for the vulnerable—someone who would step in to restore what was lost, protect the family line, and cover a widow with honor. Boaz did this for Ruth, lifting her from poverty and isolation into belonging and covenant love. His tender redemption served as a foreshadowing of Christ, our great Redeemer, who covers us with grace, restores our identity, and brings us into His family forever. Boaz's actions whispered the shape of Jesus's heart—rescuing the overlooked, restoring the broken, and rewriting stories marked by loss.

From forlorn to restored, Ruth's story whispers this hope: God writes redemption into the chapters we thought were over.

How has God written redemption into a chapter of your life that you thought was over?

Together, we have witnessed this same redeeming kindness three generations later in King David's treatment of Mephibosheth. By all cultural expectations, Sheth should have been eliminated—but David sought him out. David's compassion mirrors the heart of our King.

Now let's rejoin Sheth, standing on the threshold of the greatest restoration of his life!

Reread today's Focus Scripture, 2 Samuel 9:9-10 (page 107). Then put a check mark beside all that was given to Sheth.

____the royal land that once belonged to King Saul

____Ziba and his fifteen sons

____his grandfather's twenty servants

____a lifetime invitation to eat at David's royal table

As we saw earlier in 2 Samuel 9:4, Sheth had been living in the house of Makir, a man whose name means "bartered"—a fitting picture of a life that felt traded down, diminished, and forgotten. Now, just a few verses later, everything has changed. Sheth has gone from destitute to restored, from obscurity to honor.

King David returned the full land inheritance of King Saul and placed Ziba's fifteen sons and twenty servants under his care to farm and manage the estate. Even if Sheth had been strong and able-bodied, he never could have handled such abundance alone. He needed help, and the king provided it lavishly. But that wasn't all. David didn't stop with land. He didn't stop with laborers. He gave Sheth a place at his royal table—a seat of belonging, dignity, and daily fellowship.

In the same way, God restores us and provides for our physical, mental, emotional, and spiritual needs—sometimes before we even recognize them. Through faith in Jesus, we are made new, and by the Holy Spirit, we are empowered to walk in righteousness. Without the Spirit's strength, we could never live out the life God calls us to—yet with Him, we flourish just as Sheth did. God's presence steadies our steps, renews our courage, and reminds us that we are never left to struggle alone.

Ruth's and Sheth's journeys share the same heartbeat of restoration. Ruth is lifted from loss into a new life through Boaz, who welcomes her into a family and a future she never imagined. Sheth, crippled and forgotten, is summoned by King David and seated at the royal table as family, not foe. Both step from the margins into belonging, not by merit but by grace.

Their stories echo into ours, reminding us that God delights in redeeming the overlooked, restoring the broken, and rewriting the stories of those who thought their chapters were closed. He lifts us from the shadows, calls us by name, and seats us at His table with a new identity shaped by His unending love.

Our King anticipates our needs before we do. He sees our future and elevates us from forgotten to favored, from broken to beloved. So cue the confetti, throw your hands toward heaven, twirl with joy, and dance down your hallway in the delight of your Redeemer King!

Reread this week's memory verse and fill in the blanks.

So let us come ________ to the throne of our gracious God. There we will receive his __________, and we will find __________ to help us when we need it.

—Hebrews 4:16

Enter into a time of worship. Scan this QR code to listen to "Raise a Hallelujah" by Bethel Music.

Write your name in the blank and let this become the blessing Jesus whispers over your heart.

Come, beloved ______________. I have prepared a forever place for you at My table. I see what was lost, and I long to restore it. I see your weakness, and I provide strength. Just as David gave Mephibosheth servants to tend his inheritance, I give you My Spirit, My people, My grace to help you walk in the fullness of what I've redeemed. You are not alone. You are not forgotten. You are Mine. Sit with Me. Feast with Me. Celebrate with Me. For I rejoice over you with singing, and My joy is your strength. Welcome home!

Now offer your response: *Jesus, . . .*

Week 3

Video Viewer Guide

1. "Do not____________." King David spoke these words to Mephibosheth, and throughout Scripture we hear this same reassurance echoed again and again—often from the mouths of angels.

2. God invites us to trust Him with whatever we _______________, even when it feels painfully______________________________.

3. Jesus uses __________________________—even the parts of our past we might want to hide or throw away.

4. Our King tenderly greets us, welcomes us, and invites us to eat at His table where there _________________ are ____________________.

5. On our own, we never will be____________________, but in His hands, we are__________ __________ ____________________.

WEEK 4

Finding Comfort and Belonging

Memory Verse

"Can a mother forget her nursing child?
Can she feel no love for the child she has borne?
But even if that were possible,
I would not forget you!
See, I have written your name on the palms of my hands."

—Isaiah 49:15-16a

Recipe of the Week

Our recipe this week is M&M Party Mix, a fun snack that will have symbolic meaning in this week's video message. My hope is that someone will volunteer to prepare this recipe and you can share it as you watch the video together.

Introduction to This Week

2 Samuel 9:11-13

Congratulations on your faithfulness on this journey. As we begin week 4, we are now halfway through our study, and this week we will see that Sheth learned—no doubt, slowly and tenderly—that even in his brokenness, he was perfectly loved just as he was. This message is for us too!

We'll read that Sheth "ate regularly at David's table" (2 Samuel 9:11b). He knew he was genuinely welcome, and that the invitation was enduring. Like Sheth, we can sense the difference between a heartfelt invitation and one that is merely lip service, mouthed from obligation. Authentic hospitality is something the soul recognizes.

Just as David welcomed Sheth, our King welcomes us to come and be filled—to rest, to breathe, to find comfort for our souls in His presence. This week, He calls us to make space for Him in our busy schedules. He longs to shield us from the fear of loss and the weariness of burnout. The One who created us delights in who we are. *He genuinely likes us.* He doesn't ask us to measure what we bring to the table, comparing ourselves with others. Instead, He wants *us*—our hearts, our presence, our trust. Simple surrender is what He desires.

This week we will find comfort and belonging as we settle into the truth that we, too, have a place at the King's table.

Day 1: Fill Your Soul

Biblical Foundations:
2 Samuel 9:11a-b; Luke 22:19; John 6:35-58; Galatians 5:22-23

Focus Scripture:
Ziba replied, "Yes, my lord the king; I am your servant, and I will do all that you have commanded." And from that time on, Mephibosheth ate regularly at David's table.
—2 Samuel 9:11a-b

Welcome to the king's table! Today we're invited to sit beside Mephibosheth and savor every good thing as we taste and see that our King, Jesus, is good!

After getting settled in Jerusalem, Mephibosheth didn't *need* to eat at the king's table for nourishment. He had become a wealthy landowner, inheriting all his grandfather's royal fields. But I believe that his soul needed David's company—starved from years of just scraping by and feeling invisible.

When we are soul sick or physically sick, food helps sustain us; but the deeper healing often comes from knowing others care. I recently experienced this firsthand. During the first weeks of writing this study, I was rushed to the hospital for the first time in my life. What I assumed was a stubborn cold turned out to be viral pneumonia. After I was released, friends and family flooded me with texts and offers to bring meals. Their love mattered as much as the food.

We all need community. Sheth needed community. After years of hiding in fear, he was finally welcomed into a family, a royal family, who embraced him despite his brokenness. In the same way, our King invites us into His royal family, desiring not only to provide food for us but also to share life with us.

Reread today's Focus Scripture (above). How often did Mephibosheth eat at the king's table?

Imagine spending your life trying not to draw attention to yourself, always careful not to overstep your place as a disabled man living in the house of someone whose very name means "bartered." Mephibosheth likely had known only a sparse, humble table in Lo-debar, a land with no pastures. Suddenly, he was brought into a land of milk and honey, overflowing with abundance, where food was rich, varied, and plentiful. And he was invited to eat *regularly* at that plentiful table!

As it was for most people of his day, bread had been the center of every meal before Sheth received the royal invitation. We learned last week that for the poor, bread was often made from barley, the same grain used to feed animals. But at the king's table, there were likely many grains to choose from, and meat was no rarity. For Sheth, sitting at the most honored table in all the land must have felt like stepping into a dream. The feast before him surely filled more than his stomach; it must have nourished his soul to finally be welcomed and seen—two gifts he likely had never known.

I imagine David smiling as he slid an enormous platter of lamb toward Sheth, his voice rich with welcome: "Eat all you want!" Perhaps Mephibosheth sampled new delicacies, or maybe he clung to the familiar, as I do. With David's nineteen sons also invited to the table, it had to be laden with hearty food and surrounded by lively conversation. (As a mother of sons, I can't help wondering what their table manners were like!)

Curious about what such a royal meal might include, I did some research. Allow me to paint an imaginative scene drawing upon what I discovered. In the center of the room is a candlelit, wrought-iron chandelier above a long, low wooden table. Cushioned leather mats encircle it, inviting guests to sit cross-legged. On the table is the most enticing spread in all of ancient Israel. Picture warm, honey-drizzled breads stacked high, bowls of plump figs and glossy dates, creamy cheeses nestled beside olives glistening in golden oil, and pitchers of red wine catching the torchlight. Add roasted mutton, tender cuts of beef, fragrant lentil dishes, and clusters of fresh grapes, and it's a royal feast. Mephibosheth must have been overwhelmed by the variety set before him. One thing is certain: When he tasted the unfamiliar meats, he couldn't have said, "Tastes like chicken," because chicken didn't become part of Israel's diet until it was introduced after the Babylonian exile.[1]

At King David's royal table, there were no forks—only hands, bread, and shared bowls. Flatbread was served with a scoop, a spoon, and even a napkin, as guests reached together into savory stews and roasted meats. David's feast was communal, earthy, and intimate. I imagine it felt less like a stiff state dinner and more like a lively family gathering where everyone left full and content—maybe needing to loosen their sashes a bit.

As one accustomed to barley bread being the main course, what do you imagine Sheth might have thought and felt at King David's table?

Look up John 6:35-58. How does Jesus describe himself in these verses, and what does this communicate to you?

Even though Jesus repeatedly explained that He was the bread of life, we learn that His disciples found it difficult to understand. They ate bread daily, yet Jesus's claim to be the "bread" who satisfies the deepest hunger of the soul was a stretch for them.

For me, salvation is like warm, heavenly bread placed into our hands the moment we believe. There's no need to gather ingredients, preheat the oven, or prove our skill in the kitchen. Jesus simply offers Himself—fully baked, fully given—and our hungry heart is fed. Salvation isn't a loaf we labor to make; it's a gift received, the beautiful beginning of life with Him.

He took some bread and gave thanks to God for it. Then he broke it in pieces and gave it to the disciples, saying, "This is my body, which is given for you. Do this in remembrance of me."

—Luke 22:19

Read Luke 22:19 in the margin. What emotion do you feel when you realize He chooses to nourish you rather than demand that you fend for your own needs?

We know this command is important, for it's given to us in all three of the Synoptic Gospels (see also Matthew 26:26-28 and Mark 14:22-24). Jesus wants us to remember that He gave his body for us. He is the "bread" of eternal life. He wants us to never forget to come to Him—to fill our souls. He doesn't ask we do anything to earn our salvation. He just wants us to gather in community and remember how much He loves us.

In remembrance of Jesus, we celebrate Holy Communion together as His church family when we break bread together. This knits us together as a church family. It fills our souls, reminding us that we belong and are loved. We are accepted and invited to our King's table, just as Sheth was invited to King David's table. Jesus invites you and me to come and let Him fill our souls!

Enter into a time of worship. Scan this QR code to listen to "No Longer Slaves" by Bethel Music.

Reread this week's memory verse.

"Can a mother forget her nursing child?
Can she feel no love for the child she has borne?
But even if that were possible,
I would not forget you!
See, I have written your name on the palms of my hands."

—Isaiah 49:15-16

What stands out to you in this verse?

Write your name in the blank and let this become the blessing Jesus whispers over your heart.

Beloved __________________, come to Me and let My peace settle over you as I fill your soul with the Bread of Life that strengthens, steadies, and satisfies the places that feel empty. I will nourish every weary place within you. Let My presence become the warmth that sustains you—the daily grace that satisfies your deepest hunger. As you rise from this place, let my Bread of Life continue to shape you. Please carry my love into the world.

Now offer your response: *Jesus, . . .*

Day 2: Rest Your Soul

Biblical Foundations:
2 Samuel 9:11b; Zephaniah 3:17; Matthew 11:28; Luke 12:6-7

Focus Scripture:
Ziba replied, "Yes, my lord the king; I am your servant, and I will do all that you have commanded." And from that time on, Mephibosheth ate regularly at David's table, like one of the king's own sons.

—2 Samuel 9:11b

Yesterday we nourished our souls with the Bread of Life. Today we will find rest for our souls at our King's table, just as I imagine Sheth found rest at King David's table. I imagine David smiling so wide it showed in his eyes when he looked across the table at Mephibosheth, because he likely recognized some of Jonathan's features.

Reread today's Focus Scripture above and underline the last phrase. What does this tell us about how Sheth was treated?

I wonder if Sheth had his dad's dimples or bushy eyebrows. Perhaps he had some of Jonathan's mannerisms. Did his voice sound familiar? No doubt David was looking for glimpses of his cherished friend.

We remember our friends' faces. We remember how they smile and talk. We may even remember their quirks. Likely, David remembered these things. And chances are that when David saw Jonathan's features in Sheth, he offered a warm smile followed by a rumbling chortle as he looked for more similarities.

It makes me smile to imagine the kindness at David's table, where Sheth could rest his weary legs in quiet comfort. So often, the things we fret about most are the very things others barely notice. I certainly can fret over my hair on a bad hair day!

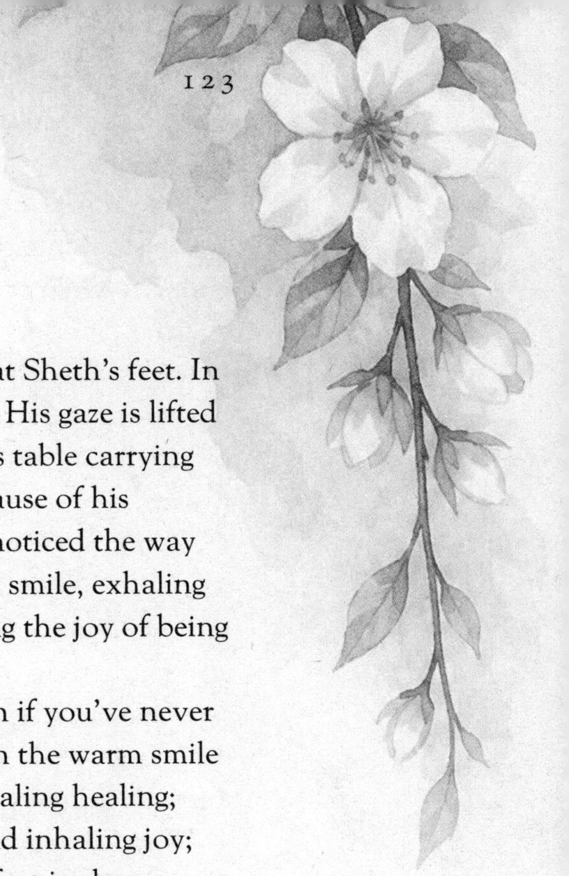

What do you fret about that others barely notice?

I'm quite sure David never once stopped eating to gaze at Sheth's feet. In the same way, our King isn't fixated on our brokenness. His gaze is lifted to our faces. Mephibosheth likely approached the king's table carrying the weight of every label society had placed on him because of his disability. But I imagine those insecurities melted as he noticed the way David looked at him. I picture Sheth soaking in David's smile, exhaling years of grief over the father he never knew and inhaling the joy of being welcomed as a child.

We can trust that our King does the same for us. Even if you've never experienced the love of an earthly father, you can rest in the warm smile of your heavenly Father—exhaling brokenness and inhaling healing; exhaling worry and inhaling peace; exhaling sadness and inhaling joy; exhaling rejection and inhaling love. At His table, comfort is always waiting. He doesn't simply love you—He *likes* you. He delights in who you are.

Read Zephaniah 3:17 in the margin. What image or memory does this bring to mind for you?

Meditate on this verse for a few moments as you breathe deeply, inhaling God's delight and exhaling self-judgment. (Set a timer for 1–2 minutes if you like.) Describe how you feel afterward:

"For the LORD your God is living among you.
He is a mighty savior.
He will take delight in you with gladness.
With his love, he will calm all your fears.
He will rejoice over you with joyful songs."

—Zephaniah 3:17

I've often heard these "songs" referred to as lullabies. Some of the sweetest moments in my life were those I spent singing lullabies over my children when they were young.

When my son Garrett was a toddler, I always knew exactly where to find him at church on a Sunday morning. He'd toddle off with great purpose, head straight for the refreshment table, snag a cookie in each of his chubby little hands, and then vanish underneath the table like a tiny raccoon.

Thinking he was completely hidden, every so often his small hand would sneak out from beneath the tablecloth to feel around and snag another cookie. Garrett assumed that because he couldn't see anyone else's face, they couldn't see him. He had what child psychologists call "egocentric sight without object permanence." Object permanence describes a child's inability to understand that things continue to exist even when they can't be seen.

Why am I sharing this? Because sometimes we make a similar mistake with our heavenly King. Because we can't physically see His face and struggle to delight in ourselves, we assume He doesn't delight in us. But that assumption is no truer than my son believing he was invisible simply because he hid his eyes.

Garrett was fully seen by the "cookie ladies." In fact, he brought them joy. They lovingly placed cookies within his reach. They watched over him as he "hid." They treasured how he stashed cookies in his suit jacket pockets.

Similarly, our heavenly King watches over us and delights in us. We don't need to hide under the table as my son once did. We can pull up a chair and dine with our King. We are precious in His sight and bring Him great joy.

Read Luke 12:6-7 in the margin. Which phrase in these verses touches your heart?

> "What is the price of five sparrows—two copper coins? Yet God does not forget a single one of them. And the very hairs on your head are all numbered. So don't be afraid; you are more valuable to God than a whole flock of sparrows."
>
> ***—Luke 12:6-7***

My mom quoted this verse often when I was a child. I knew God's Word was true, so occasionally I would pluck a hair from my head just to make sure God was keeping watch over me. I'd lift it high like a tiny antenna, hoping He'd catch the signal and wink back, confirming I wasn't invisible after all. Even though I didn't feel pretty at school, I knew my parents thought I was pretty. This calmed my soul and allowed me to smile, something I avoided in public because of my broken front tooth.

> Then Jesus said, "Come to me, all of you who are weary and carry heavy burdens, and I will give you rest."
>
> ***—Matthew 11:28***

Read Matthew 11:28 in the margin. Based on this verse, mark each statement with T (True) or F (False).

_____ Come to me when you deserve me.

_____ Come to me when you have your act together.

_____ Come to me when you aren't consumed with fear.

_____ Come to me when you are tired, need rest, and need help carrying heavy burdens

As we end our day together, reflect on what you need help carrying this week. Remember, God invites us to come as we are, lay down our burdens, and allow him to delight in us and sing over us. Then we will find rest for our souls!

Reread this week's memory verse and fill in the blank.

"Can a mother forget her nursing ________ ?
Can she feel no love for the child she has borne?
But even if that were possible,
I would not forget you!
See, I have written your name on the palms of my hands."
—Isaiah 49:15-16

Enter into a time of worship. Scan this QR code to listen to "Hello, My Name Is" by Matthew West.

Write your name in the blank and let this become the blessing Jesus whispers over your heart.

Come ______________, My beloved. Draw near and sit at My table. Let your soul bask in the warmth of My approval. I do not merely love you—I delight in you. Rest here with Me. Lay down the weight of trying, and let My presence fill you with quiet contentment. You are safe in My company, cherished in My gaze, and wanted at My table. Stay a while. Let My joy become your rest.

Now offer your response: Jesus, . . .

Day 3: Rest from Fear of Loss

Biblical Foundations:
Deuteronomy 31:6; 2 Samuel 9:12a; Daniel 3:16-18, 25; Ephesians 6:12; 1 Peter 5:8

Focus Scripture:
Mephibosheth had a young son named Mica. —2 Samuel 9:12a

At the innocent age of five, Mephibosheth lost his entire family. Hidden away in Lo-debar in fear, he surely grieved that loss and wondered if he would belong to any family again. Yet here in 2 Samuel 9:12, we're told an interesting fact, almost as a side note.

In today's "Focus Scripture" above, draw a circle around the name of Mephibosheth's son.

Mephibosheth had a young son named Mica. This mention of Mica is no small thing but carries remarkable weight.

What do you think is the significance of Mica's mention here?

Mica's presence in Scripture shows that Jonathan's family line did not end with Mephibosheth, even after Saul's tragic downfall. God used Mica's life to fulfill the covenant David had made with Jonathan—to show steadfast kindness to his descendants (1 Samuel 20:14-17). In a story marked by loss, upheaval, and the collapse of a royal household, Mica stands as a quiet thread of preservation woven by God's faithful hand.

Mica becomes a symbol of hope. His very existence testifies that God's mercy does not evaporate when circumstances crumble. Instead, His kindness continues to flow through generations, often in ways that are subtle but deeply significant. Many interpret the God of the Old Testament as distant and unkind, but the truth is that God has always cared deeply for His children. We see that in Mephibosheth's story.

David's covenant loyalty did not stop with Mephibosheth, reminding us that God's promises ripple outward farther than we can see. What looked like the end of a family line was, in God's eyes, simply the beginning of restoration. Mica grew up not in the shadows of shame but in a place where grace was practiced, not merely promised.

What are the quiet or surprising ways God has carried your family?

Mica's life reminds us of faithfulness across generations. God's promises don't expire when life becomes bleak. His covenant love stretches beyond the moment we're in, reaching children and grandchildren we may never meet. Mica also reflects David's covenant loyalty—a human echo of divine kindness. Even his name is a living testimony to God's glory.

The name Mica comes from the Hebrew Mîkā (a shortened form of Mîkhāyāh), which means "Who is like Yahweh?"[2] It's a rhetorical question, not expecting an answer, because the implied truth is that no one compares to the Lord. In Scripture, names often carry identity and destiny, and so Mica's name is a quiet proclamation of God's unmatched greatness. It serves as a reminder of God's uniqueness, a declaration of divine supremacy, and a whisper of worship woven into a family line marked by both tragedy and grace. In a household restored by covenant kindness, Mica's name testified daily that the God who preserves, restores, and redeems is utterly without equal.

Reflecting on that kind of grace draws me back to my own story, to a season when fear pressed hard against my trust. My son Garrett was young when I began having dreams of him drowning. In my dream, I saw him floating face down in our backyard pool. Some nights I would bolt awake, my heart pounding. I'd whisper an apology to my husband for waking him and then slip out of our bedroom and cross the hall to check on Garrett. There he always was, safe and peaceful with his pointer finger resting beside his pudgy little nose.

Despite the fact that I was awake, it was hard to forget the image of my son floating face down. Though I knew that I had locked the back door before bed and set the alarm, I'd still find myself hurrying to the living room to check it again. I'd flood the room with light, then open my Bible to flood my mind with the Light of God's Word.

Has your mind ever painted a picture that your heart couldn't ignore? If so, describe it below.

Once again, I recognized the familiar signs of panic attacks that came hand in hand with these nightmares. As a pharmacist, I understood the physiology behind them, yet knowledge didn't stop the experience. Like a stealth bomber, fear slipped into my dreams, dropping its fury like bombs.

Although my dream was specific, I'm not alone in fearing the loss of someone I love to death or illness. "Fear of loss" is natural and one of the top five most common stress-inducing fears that attack women.[3]

Overcoming my fear of loss required supernatural help. Here are three of my favorite verses that have helped me to supernaturally fight fear over the years.

Draw a line from each verse on the left to its corresponding text on the right.

1 Peter 5:8	"So be strong and courageous! Do not be afraid and do not panic before them. For the LORD your God will personally go ahead of you. He will neither fail you nor abandon you."
Ephesians 6:12	For we are not fighting against flesh-and-blood enemies, but against evil rulers and authorities of the unseen world, against mighty powers in this dark world, and against evil spirits in the heavenly places.
Deuteronomy 31:6	Stay alert! Watch out for your great enemy, the devil. He prowls around like a roaring lion, looking for someone to devour.

Each night when terror jolted me awake, I would switch on the lamp above the comfy wingback chair where I've always met God in His Word. There, I turned to the Light of Scripture until my mind was filled with what is true, right, noble, and pure—principles we explored in Philippians 4:8 earlier in our study. Slowly, fear loosened its grip and my breathing steadied.

I reminded myself that God loves my children more perfectly than I ever could. And as much as I longed to shield them from every harm, that was impossible. So instead of bartering with God—as I had done before when I thought I had breast cancer—I surrendered them into His care. My continual prayer was simple: "God, I know You love them more perfectly than I ever could, and I entrust them into Your care. *Even if* harm should come, I know that in the end, You hold them safely in Your arms."

I'm not the first to pray an "even if" prayer; a faith declaration. Perhaps you've prayed one too. Let's take a look at one of the best examples of an "even if" faith proclamation found in the story of Shadrach, Meshach, and Abednego and the fiery furnace.

In Daniel 3, we read that Nebuchadnezzar built a huge golden statue and ordered everyone to bow to it when the music played. Shadrach, Meshach, and Abednego refused, angering the king. He threatened to throw them into a blazing furnace if they didn't worship the idol, demanding their obedience.

Read Daniel 3:16-18 and paraphrase their "even if" proclamation to the king.

Now continue reading verses 19-25. What did Nebuchadnezzar do to them before he threw them in the furnace? And what happened next?

Commentators agree that it was the preincarnate Christ Himself who stood in the fire with them. Shadrach, Meshach, and Abednego were thrown into the furnace bound, yet the only thing the fire destroyed was the ropes that *bound* them. Let that truth free your soul!

Just as I had to release to God my fear of losing my child, what fear might God be inviting you to surrender so that its grip no longer holds you captive?

Jesus walks with you through every fearful trial just as He walked with me when I feared losing my son. I knew God understood my fear of loss. After all, He lost His beloved Son—but even then, evil lost. Good triumphed. We aren't promised a life free from fiery trials, but we're promised the faithful presence of Jesus beside us in every flame. We never walk alone—and our good God will triumph over every foe that comes against us.

Reread this week's memory verse and fill in the blanks:

"Can a mother forget her nursing __________?

Can she feel no _______ for the child she has borne?

But even if that were possible,

I would not forget you!

See, I have written your name on the palms of my hands."

— Isaiah 49:15-16

Enter into a time of worship. Scan this QR code to listen to "Even If" by MercyMe.

Write your name in the blank and let this become the blessing Jesus whispers over your heart.

My beloved________________, surrender your fear of loss. Even if flames surround you, I am with you. Even if the answer doesn't come the way you imagined, I am still good. I am still yours. Choose to trust Me—not only when I deliver, but even when I ask you to wait and rest in Me. Evil will not win; I have overcome. My love endures forever. You are never abandoned, never unseen. Let go of what you fear to lose. I will restore, redeem, and rejoice over you with singing. You are Mine. Always.

Now offer your "Even If" prayer (it may be one of the most freeing prayers you will ever pray): *Jesus, . . .*

Day 4: Rest from Busyness and Burnout

Biblical Foundations:
2 Samuel 9:12b; Luke 10:38-42

Focus Scripture:
From then on, all the members of Ziba's household were Mephibosheth's servants.
—2 Samuel 9:12b

When someone asks how you are, have you ever answered by saying you're busy? Busy may describe your schedule or even your season, but it doesn't define you. It's often wisely said, We are human *beings*, not human *doings*.

As women who work both inside and outside our homes, we often confuse our worth with what we accomplish. So we do more. And then we try to do it more perfectly. It's impossible. And it leads to busyness and burnout.

There's a story in Scripture about two sisters I've long called the "M&M Sisters." I love M&M's, but I love these women more. I see pieces of myself both in Mary and Martha.

As a writer who loves words, I can't help noticing that both names begin with the same three letters: M-a-r. This feels significant to me, because I can start my week with the heart of Mary—sitting, listening, and even serving from a place of peace. But three days in, I often find that my serving, my tongue, and my attitude begin to slip. And I become more like Martha—worried, cumbered, and pulled in many directions. What began well takes a hard left the moment I notice everything that's undone, everything that needs to be redone, and everything that will never get done. After all, someone has to take care of business (not to be confused with busyness).

It's time to look at Mary and Martha through the compassionate eyes of Jesus—to set aside the labels we've placed on them and let Jesus's gaze show us who they truly are. Martha wasn't scolded for serving; she was invited to breathe. She wasn't dismissed; she was seen. Perhaps the real invitation for every modern Martha, every overextended woman, is to let go of the pressure to manage everything and step into the presence that steadies everything.

> As Jesus and the disciples continued on their way to Jerusalem, they came to a certain village where a woman named Martha welcomed him into her home. Her sister, Mary, sat at the Lord's feet, listening to what he taught.
>
> ***—Luke 10:38-39***

Read Luke 10:38-39 in the margin. Which sister is named first?

Because Martha is named first, and because she is the one who welcomes Jesus and His disciples into her home, she may have been the eldest. Her sister, Mary, sat at Jesus's feet, fully engaged and actively listening. This alone was remarkable. In that culture, only men typically sat at a rabbi's feet. For Jesus to welcome Mary into that space broke through the expected norms of the day. Mary was not passively lounging; she was actively learning.

When teaching on this passage, I like to invite women to step into the tension between these two sisters so they can *feel* the story rather than simply *read* it. At conferences, I ask them to pair up—one woman assuming the role of Martha, and the other woman assuming the role of Mary. Then I give Martha a challenge: Communicate everything she's thinking using only her face and body. No words allowed. Oh, the sermons our faces can preach!

I imagine Martha starting with the classic stink eye aimed at Mary, followed by the side-eye, and then the sharp finger-curling "come here" motion toward the kitchen. All of this while silently mouthing the unmistakable message: "*Mary, get in here now and help me!*" Long before Martha ever approached Jesus, her whole body was already screaming at Mary.

Read Luke 10:40. What did Martha tell Jesus to do?

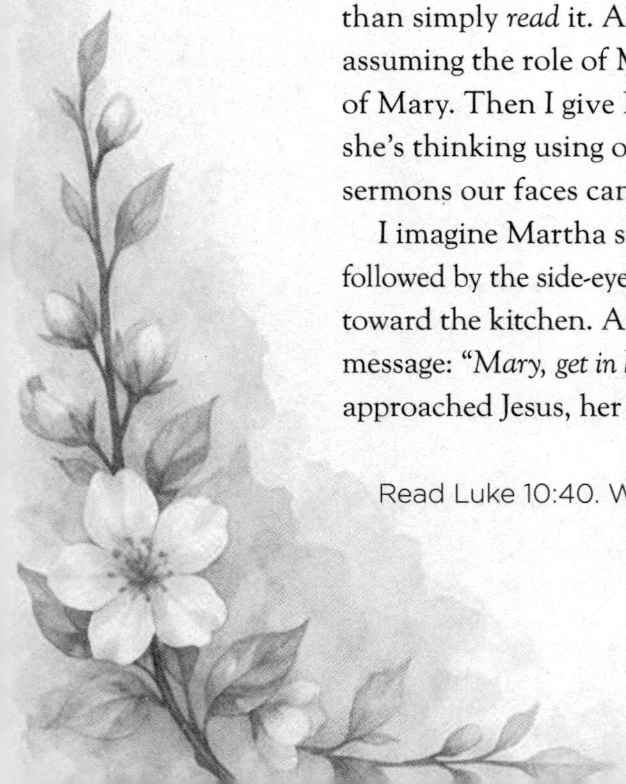

I can't help smiling, because I've done the exact same thing—marched right up to the Creator of the universe with my own step-by-step plan for how He should fix my situation ASAP. It's like handing God a to-do list and saying, "If You could initial at the bottom, that'd be great." And yet, Jesus never rolls His eyes or sighs dramatically. He simply responds with that same gentle, steadying grace He offered Martha.

Now read Luke 10:41-42. Place a check mark next to the tone of voice you imagine Jesus used.

_____ angry
_____ frustrated
_____ condescending
_____ tender

In the New Living Translation (Luke 10:41), Jesus says, "My dear Martha," using a term of endearment. In other translations, he repeats her name twice. This tells us Jesus sees Martha and is attentive and tender. He isn't condescending. He's compassionate. He isn't angry and short. He sees the busyness and burnout written in the furrow of her brow. He names what He sees—worry and upset—because He knows how easily a heart can get tangled in the details.

When we become distracted by the details, what began as service offered with a merry heart slowly shifts into service done with a burdened heart—and that burden leads straight to the dead end of busyness and burnout.

When have you become distracted by the details and found yourself shifting toward a burdened heart?

Jesus isn't saying that *serving* is less honorable than *learning*. He's saying that being worried and burdened is not what He wants for us.

When I think about my own life, there are several factors that influence my heart attitude while serving. Below are a few. Place a check mark beside the ones that most often lead to a cumbered heart when you serve:

_____ lack of sleep
_____ caregiving responsibilities
_____ mental load of managing the household
_____ workplace pressures and expectations
_____ safety concerns and constant mental vigilance
_____ other: ____
____

With a focus on serving, let's return to Sheth's story.

Reread today's Focus Scripture, 2 Samuel 9:12b (page 133). Write the last word below and circle the last letter.

Sheth used this word in its singular form earlier when he said to David, "I am your servant." Today we see David use the same word in its plural form, but this time, David is providing the servants. This is important.

Mephibosheth inherited King Saul's land, but he never would have had the manpower to farm it had David not assigned Saul's former servants (plural) to help. Ziba alone had fifteen sons and twenty servants. Having served in the royal court, this new assignment may have felt like a setback to Ziba. We'll consider that more closely next week. But for now, here's an important application for us: God knows we can't do everything on our own without it leading to busyness and burnout, and He offers us rest.

As we close today's study, take a few well-deserved moments to rest. Remember that Jesus invites us—as He did Martha—to breathe, unwind, and gently step back from busyness and burnout.

Reread this week's memory verse and fill in the blanks.

"Can a mother forget her nursing __________?

Can she feel no _______ for the child she has borne?

But even if that were ________________,

I would not forget you!

See, I have written your name on the palms of my hands."

—Isaiah 49:15-16

Enter into a time of worship. Scan this QR code to listen to "Come Alive" by Lauren Daigle.

Write your name in the blank and let this become the blessing Jesus whispers over your heart.

Beloved ________________, I see your every hidden effort, every quiet act of care, every small choice to bless another. Nothing you offer in love is ever unnoticed by Me. Stay close to My heart, for it keeps your focus steady and your spirit at rest. I take delight every time you refuse to let the details pull you away from what matters most. Walk in the gentle strength of My presence. Let My peace guard your thoughts as you serve. I am with you, rejoicing over your faithfulness.

Now offer your response: *Jesus, . . .*

Day 5: Rest from Comparison

Biblical Foundations:
Genesis 1:31a; 2 Samuel 9:13; Ephesians 2:10; 1 Peter 2:9; 3:3-4

Focus Scripture:
And Mephibosheth, who was crippled in both feet, lived in Jerusalem and ate regularly at the king's table. —2 Samuel 9:13

When I was in fifth grade, I remember sitting next to my friend Susie in the lunchroom. I glanced at her legs, then down at my own, pressed wide against the cold metal chair. A single thought flashed through my mind with painful clarity: "My legs are fat. I wish my legs were skinny like Susie's legs."

That afternoon, as my siblings and I sat at the kitchen table enjoying our after-school snack, I casually mentioned to my mom that I thought my legs were fat. She immediately stood up, walked over to my chair, and knelt before me so her eyes were level with mine. Her voice was tender but intentional. "Lisa, you have beautiful, shapely legs. Your legs work. You can walk and run. You are fearfully and wonderfully made." Then with the authority that comes from speaking truth, she decreed, "Never again do I want to hear you criticize your body."

I didn't realize at the time that my mom was echoing Psalm 139:14, which says we are fearfully and wonderfully made. But I could hear in her voice that what she spoke was meant to stand like a monument of truth—a boundary she would not let me cross. God had made me, and I was not to speak against His handiwork.

My makeshift bedroom was just off the kitchen, closed off by an ugly, green sliding vinyl door my dad had installed. After leaving the table that day, I pulled the accordion door shut and stood in front of my dresser mirror looking at my legs, turning over my mom's words.

I was a tween then, and her admonition has stayed with me ever since. In fact, I used the same Bible verse with my daughter when she was a tween and compared herself to others. It's so easy to look at peers and want their bodies or their lives. Comparison creeps into our souls and settles like dust on furniture that once gleamed. How my mom responded that day reshaped the role that comparison would play in my life.

With comparison as a backdrop for today's lesson, let's return to Sheth's story.

Reread today's Focus Scripture, 2 Samuel 9:13, above. What stands out to you in this passage?

I love the last phrase—which repeats for the second time in just a few verses—that Mephibosheth is now eating "regularly at the king's table." With equal emotion, I dislike the phrase "who was crippled in both feet." I dislike the connotation that the word *crippled* carries and much prefer the word *disabled*. We each have abilities and disabilities. We each have strengths and weaknesses, talents and untapped potentials. Physically, emotionally, and spiritually, we're each unique.

So often we fixate on the negative, on what we believe is broken or imperfect in our own appearance. Think about how you look at a photo of yourself—do your eyes go straight to the features you wish were different? Without thinking, we compare ourselves to edited images on social media and television, forgetting that those standards aren't real. We demand flawlessness from ourselves, even though we're human and inherently limited. Maybe that's the point of Sheth's disability that affects *both* feet: it reminds us that neither our abilities nor our limitations defines our worth. Our brokenness doesn't disqualify us, and our gifts don't make us more deserving. We are all welcome at the King's table exactly as we are.

You are a chosen people. You are royal priests, a holy nation, God's very own possession. As a result, you can show others the goodness of God, for he called you out of the darkness into his wonderful light.

—1 Peter 2:9

Read 1 Peter 2:9 in the margin. Which part of this verse do you find most affirming today?

Let's again imagine King David's banquet hall. First, find Sheth at the table. Who else would Sheth see sitting there? What conversations might he hear?

He might hear the confident voice of David's son Solomon—the man the Bible calls the wisest to ever live (1 Kings 10:23-24)—rising above the others as he debated ethics and deeper understanding with anyone willing to engage him. Nearby might be the strikingly handsome Absalom, his luxurious hair catching the candlelight. David's other sons would surely be present as well, each granted a place at the royal table by virtue of the blood that ran through their veins.

Close to the king might sit Joab, commander of David's army, his battlefield stories unmatched. The leaders of David's mighty men—Shammah, Josheb, and Eleazar—could have joined the conversation when in Jerusalem reporting to the king. It makes me smile to imagine them picking up the serving knives and wielding them like swords as they reenact their acts of valor!

The high priest would likely appear as an honored guest occasionally, along with Nathan the prophet and trusted advisors like Hushai and Ahithophel. Scribes, valued for their wisdom and guardianship of the Law, may also have been present. And at times, the table may have echoed with many languages, as foreign rulers and dignitaries joined by diplomatic invitation.

Mephibosheth, however, would have stood out because he could not easily stand up. Saul's and Jonathan's blood flowed through his veins, and he was seated at the king's table by virtue of Jonathan and David's covenant love. In a similar way, we have been invited to our King's table by virtue of the blood and covenant love of our friend, Jesus.

David called Mephibosheth into the light of his family. Sheth could have shrunken from the king's table had he allowed comparison to settle in his heart. It would have been understandable. After all, Sheth's legs were likely shriveled, his muscles atrophied from lack of use. He may have looked down at his legs with contempt as he sat next to mighty military men who were strong commanders.

Consider this. If you were Sheth—sitting among able-bodied men—would you have been tempted to look down at your feeble legs and compare them to the others' strong legs? I was vulnerable when I compared my "fat" legs to Susie's "skinny" legs. Every one of us is vulnerable to the trap of comparison. That's why we must fix our eyes on Jesus, not on others, and refuse to measure ourselves against anyone else.

If you've ever compared yourself to others and questioned why God made you the way He did or wondered what He thinks of you, this verse answers both of these life-shaping questions.

Read Ephesians 2:10 in the margin and fill in the blanks below, speaking God's truth aloud over yourself. If you have a mirror nearby, consider declaring these truths while looking at your reflection.

I am God's ______________________________.

I am created for______________________________.

For we are God's masterpiece. He has created us anew in Christ Jesus, so we can do the good things he planned for us long ago.

—Ephesians 2:10

If you still have a tinge of doubt when you look in the mirror, be comforted with these words from our Creator.

Read Genesis 1:31a in the margin and circle God's assessment.

God saw all that he had made, and it was very good.

—Genesis 1:31a NIV

The phrase for "very good" in Hebrew is *tov me'od*, and it paints a picture far richer than our English words. The word *tov* speaks of something that is good in the deepest sense—beautiful, life-giving, and functioning exactly as it was designed. Then *me'od* comes alongside and pours abundance over it, meaning "exceedingly," "overflowingly," "to the fullest extent."[4]

Together, *tov me'od* describes creation not just as good but as good in perfect harmony—every part aligned with God's purpose, every relationship in right order, everything complete and whole. It's the moment when God looks at His work and sees not only goodness but also goodness fulfilled.

As women, we tend to be incredibly hard on ourselves—especially when it comes to our appearance. We compare ourselves to AI-enhanced photos online that can make us feel small because they show "perfect" women who don't actually exist—flawless faces, flawless lives, all polished by technology. It's easy to start comparing ourselves to those pretend versions without realizing it.

Spiritually, we sometimes do the same thing when we compare ourselves to the Proverbs 31 woman—an acrostic portrait that King Lemuel painted from his mother's teachings (Proverbs 31:1), not a measuring stick for us. When we compare ourselves to AI perfection or the Proverbs 31 woman, we can end up discouraged. Real freedom comes when we embrace the beautifully real, grace-filled women we already are.

Can you recall a time recently when you compared yourself to images online? How did that make you feel?

Have you ever compared yourself to the Proverbs 31 woman—or a spiritual woman you admire? If so, how did that make you feel?

When we stop measuring ourselves against others, we discover the quiet miracle of being exactly whom God designed us to be. *Comparison* drains us; *calling* restores us. The moment we release the need to "keep up," we become free to "look up"—and that is where strength returns.

***Comparison* drains us; *calling* restores us.**

Read 1 Peter 3:3-4 in the margin. What matters and what doesn't? What are we to cultivate?

What matters is not your outer appearance—the styling of your hair, the jewelry you wear, the cut of your clothes—but your inner disposition. Cultivate inner beauty, the gentle, gracious kind that God delights in.

—1 Peter 3:3-4 MSG

As we close this week of study, let me congratulate you once more. For four weeks, you have diligently immersed yourself in God's Word. You have purposely set aside time dedicated to spiritual growth. You are *becoming*—beautifully, intentionally, and in God's perfect timing. Keep going. Our King must smile as He looks at your heart.

You are a wise woman of faith who understands that outer beauty wanes while inner beauty reigns. So let's step out of the shadow of comparison and into the light of God's delight. He isn't asking us to be better than anyone else; He's inviting us to become the truest version of ourselves. And as we walk in that freedom, we give other women permission to do the same. The world needs the story only *you* can live!

Outer beauty wanes while inner beauty reigns.

Reread this week's memory verse and fill in the blanks.

"Can a mother forget her nursing __________?

Can she feel no _______ for the child she has borne?

But even if that were ___________________,

I would not forget you!

See, I have written your name on the _______________

of my hands."

—Isaiah 49:15-16

Enter into a time of worship. Scan this QR code to listen to "Redeemed" by Big Daddy Weave.

Write your name in the blank and let this become the blessing Jesus whispers over your heart.

Beloved________________, do not let comparison steal your joy or settle on your soul like dust in the sunlight. I formed you with delight and intention. You are My masterpiece, created for good works that carry your unique imprint. You do not need to twist yourself into the pretzel-shapes of others' expectations. I love the way I made you. Let My gaze be the mirror you trust. In My eyes, you are radiant, chosen, and wonderfully made.

Now offer your response: *Jesus, . . .*

Week 4

Video Viewer Guide

1. Mary's posture is not ________________; it is ______________________.
   Jesus honors her hunger for truth and dignifies her desire to learn.

2. Martha moves quickly, thinks practically, and expresses ______________
   through__________________.

3. Jesus wasn't correcting Martha's activity; He was addressing her anxiety. He wasn't rejecting her service; He was ____________________ _____ _________.

4. Our growth comes from __________________ in God, not __________________ to prove our worth.

5. Comparison steals our____________________, while looking to God restores our peace.

6. God invites us out of ____________________ and into ______________.

7. We are invited not to _____ more, but to ______________ more deeply at the King's table.

WEEK 5

Living in an Imperfect World

Memory Verse

I have hidden your word in my heart,
that I might not sin against you.
I praise you, O LORD*;*
teach me your decrees.

—Psalm 119:11-12

Recipe of the Week

Like our week ahead, this recipe is tart but ends on a sweet, satisfying note. It has just four ingredients and takes only four minutes to make. And the best part? You'll only dirty one spoon. A tiny effort with a big payoff; a dessert that's quick to make and slow to forget.

Recipe Faux Key Lime Pie

INGREDIENTS

- 1 16 oz. tub softened Cool Whip
- 1 7 oz. can sweetened condensed milk
- 1 package lemon-lime Kool-Aid
- 1 graham cracker crust
- *Optional:* fresh lime slices

DIRECTIONS

1. Add sweetened condensed milk and Kool-Aid to the tub of Cool Whip and mix well; then add to the pie crust and chill.
2. *Optional* Garnish: fresh lime slices.

Introduction to This Week

2 Samuel 13–30

This is the week when Mephibosheth is swept into the crossfire of betrayal as David's once-steady dynasty trembles and loyalties shift.

Even though we're graciously invited to sit at our King's table, we, too, will face trials that stretch our faith and deepen our endurance. In the Book of James, we read, "Dear brothers and sisters, when troubles of any kind come your way, consider it an opportunity for great joy. For you know that when your faith is tested, your endurance has a chance to grow" (James 1:2-3). He didn't say *if* troubles come but *when* they come. These battles may unsettle us, even shake us, but Sheth offers us a steadying model. His humble, loyal, and anchored posture shows us what it looks like to stay faithful when the world around us tilts.

Like Sheth, we can guard our hearts, remain loyal to our King, and stay grateful for all He has done. Gratitude becomes its own kind of ballast. When our focus rests on the gifts and graces we've already received, we begin to discover a life that is quietly rich, deeply rooted, and genuinely content.

Day 1: There Will Be Battles and Betrayals

Biblical Foundations:
2 Samuel 13:1, 21, 37-39; 14:24; 16:1-4

Focus Scripture:
When David had gone a little beyond the summit of the Mount of Olives, Ziba, the servant of Mephibosheth, was waiting there for him. He had two donkeys loaded with 200 loaves of bread, 100 clusters of raisins, 100 bunches of summer fruit, and a wineskin full of wine.

"What are these for?" the king asked Ziba.

Ziba replied, "The donkeys are for the king's people to ride on, and the bread and summer fruit are for the young men to eat. The wine is for those who become exhausted in the wilderness."

"And where is Mephibosheth, Saul's grandson?" the king asked him.

"He stayed in Jerusalem," Ziba replied. "He said, 'Today I will get back the kingdom of my grandfather Saul.'"

"In that case," the king told Ziba, "I give you everything Mephibosheth owns."

"I bow before you," Ziba replied. "May I always be pleasing to you, my lord the king."
—2 Samuel 16:1-4

Some seasons are unexpectedly hard. Even though we're loved by God, we still experience difficulties in this life; potholes that are unexpected and jarring. Like Mephibosheth, who found himself caught in the middle of a kingdom divided, we, too, can be swept into conflicts we never chose.

Sometimes we can be pulled into the cross fire of fractured relationships, infidelity, abandonment, or divorce. Prodigal children or estranged siblings can result in families divided. Unhealed generational wounds can resurface. Other times, the struggle can come from financial strain, job loss, unexpected expenses, health trials, or mismanaged budgets.

Some crises arrive in an instant, like a car accident. Others creep in slowly, such as chronic health conditions that wear down our minds, bodies, and spirits. Sometimes the heavy weight of caregiving becomes unbearable. Some griefs we expect, such as aging parents or loved ones who finish their race. Others we never anticipate. In the midst of whatever trials we face, spiritual dryness is not uncommon. We may find ourselves disappointed with God, our hearts heavy with unanswered prayers, wandering through what feels like a desert of doubt.

Scripture reminds us that seasons like these are not new. They echo through the lives of those who have gone before us. If you have walked through such hardship, you can begin to understand how Sheth was swept into the chaos of a dynasty unraveling—its first thread pulled by David's lust for Bathsheba (2 Samuel 11) and the next by his son's lust for his own sister (2 Samuel 13).

Look up 2 Samuel 13 and hold your place there. Write the telling title of the chapter below.

If you haven't read this story before, I encourage you to read chapter 13. Verse 1 names the four main characters. List them below, briefly describing each one.

What did Amnon do? (vv. 6, 14)

What emotion did King David feel when he heard what happened? (v. 21)

How did Absalom feel toward Amnon, and what did he say? (v. 21)

Amnon lusted for his half-sister, Tamar, and raped her. Both David and Absalom were furious, yet they remained silent. Though David was a respected leader, he didn't lead his family well or model healthy communication. After waiting two years for his father to bring justice, Absalom finally took matters into his own hands, murdering his brother to avenge his sister.

After Absalom fled, how long did he remain in a foreign land with his grandfather? (vv. 37-38)

What did David long for? (v. 39)

At this point in the story, five years have passed since the rape of Tamar. Chapter 13 ends with David longing for reunion with Absalom, and chapter 14 tells us that David allowed Absalom to come back to Israel with one stipulation.

Turn to 2 Samuel 14:24. What was the wounding stipulation David placed on Absalom?

David's refusal to deal with Amnon's crime and Absalom's refusal to forgive his father for that set off a chain of vengeance. This culminated in Absalom killing his brother and David responding with the damaging decree that his son "must never come into my presence" (2 Samuel 14:24).

Has your family ever experienced division marked more by silence than open conflict? Explain.

Absalom grew to hate his father and sought his destruction. When he returned to Jerusalem, he positioned himself at the city gate, where disputes were heard. As people came seeking justice, Absalom intercepted them with charm and cunning. He listened, sympathized, and promised fairness. Scripture says that Absalom "stole the hearts of all the people of Israel" (2 Samuel 15:6).

David, who had once united the nation, now watched his own son quietly erode his authority. This slow betrayal, which took place over two years, was deliberate and deeply personal. What began as resentment became a full-scale coup.

Seven long years of simmering hurt between father and son erupted when Absalom crowned himself king (2 Samuel 15:7-12). Then David, the giant slayer and battlefield legend, fled his own city barefoot and weeping (2 Samuel 15:30).

Betrayals followed. David's trusted counselor, Ahithophel, sided with Absalom (2 Samuel 15:31). It's important to know that Ahithophel was the grandfather of Bathsheba—the married woman David had taken for himself many years earlier.

Bathsheba, the wife of Uriah—a brave, righteous man—had been summoned by David to his bed with no rights or power to refuse him. Though Scripture never explicitly labels David's actions as rape, the moment Ahithophel sides with Absalom reveals his justified anger over the sin committed against his granddaughter years earlier.

When sin, anger, or resentment is buried, it surfaces in ugly ways. Another betrayal followed when Ziba deceived David. In week 3 of our study, we saw that Ziba was assigned to serve in the household of Mephibosheth. I believe it's possible that Ziba held this subservient position against Sheth and, when given the opportunity, sought to supplant him, though the biblical narrative frames his actions as loyalty. Let's take a closer look at how Ziba made his move.

When sin, anger, or resentment is buried, it surfaces in ugly ways.

Reread today's Focus Scripture, 2 Samuel 16:1-4 (page 149). Ziba was working Sheth's land. So whose harvest do you suppose he was "gifting" to David?

Circle the correct answers, indicating how much was given of each:

loaves of bread:	(A) 100	(B) 200	(C) 300
clusters of raisins:	(A) 50	(B) 100	(C) 200
bunches of summer fruit:	(A) 100	(B) 200	(C) 400
donkeys:	(A) 1	(B) 2	(C) 3

Reread 2 Samuel 16:4a in the margin and circle what David gave Ziba in return.

"In that case," the king told Ziba, "I give you everything Mephibosheth owns."

—2 Samuel 16:4a

Before we hear from Sheth in tomorrow's lesson and uncover the truth, let me briefly summarize how Absalom's rebellion ended.

As Absalom fled the battlefield, his long hair became entangled in the branches of a tree, leaving him dangling (2 Samuel 18:9). Though David had pleaded for Absalom's life to be spared should he be captured, his commander, Joab, refused that order and struck Absalom down (2 Samuel 18:14-15). It's a sobering and heartbreaking story. When David heard the news, his grief was overwhelming: "O my son Absalom! My son, my son Absalom! If only I had died instead of you! O Absalom, my son, my son" (2 Samuel 18:33).

David's victory was hollow, for the cost was the life of the son he loved. Even after Absalom's death, betrayals continued to unfold. For David, each revolt served as another reminder of the betrayals his sins had set in motion.

In one way or another, we all have experienced the pain caused by betrayal. Yet as we have seen, we can take refuge in the One who sees, who fights for us, and whose love holds our victory securely.

Enter into a time of worship. Scan this QR code to listen to "Thank God I Do" by Lauren Daigle.

Reread this week's memory verse.

I have hidden your word in my heart,
that I might not sin against you.
I praise you, O Lord;
teach me your decrees.
—Psalm 119:11-12

What stands out to you in this verse?

Write your name in the blank and let this become the blessing Jesus whispers over your heart.

Beloved ________________, come to Me. I know the battles that rise against you and the betrayals that pierce your heart. Nothing touches your life without Me seeing it, and I fight for you in ways you cannot imagine. When others misjudge you or try to stain your name, remain faithful in love. Your victory is not fragile; it rests in My hands. Trust that I will lift you up at the right time. Walk forward in peace, for you are deeply, endlessly loved.

Now offer your response: *Jesus, . . .*

Day 2: Guard Your Heart

Biblical Foundations:
1 Samuel 16:7; 2 Samuel 19:24-27a; Psalm 51:10; Proverbs 4:23; Luke 6:45

Focus Scripture:
Now Mephibosheth, Saul's grandson, came down from Jerusalem to meet the king. He had not cared for his feet, trimmed his beard, or washed his clothes since the day the king left Jerusalem. —2 Samuel 19:24

In my pharmacy career, my focus was heart medications—so you could say I've had a front-row seat to the drama of the human heart. There are all kinds of tests that let us peek inside that hardworking muscle—all requiring machines, appointments, and a copay. But there's one heart checkup that's absolutely free. We can know the condition of our heart's spiritual health—and that exam doesn't require a waiting room, a hospital gown, or even a needle. Just honest reflection and a willingness to listen. Dr. Luke knew about this heart exam.

Look up Luke 6:45 and fill in the blanks:

A ________ person produces ________ things from the treasury of a ________ heart, and an ________ person produces ________ things from the treasury of an ____________ heart. What you say ________ from what is in your heart.

Recently I did an impromptu spiritual heart scan on myself—the kind you do while standing in your kitchen with a cup of coffee, wondering what's really swirling around in your soul. And as I stood there, several moments came to mind.

One day I was shuffling through the house in my cozy socks, minding my own business, when my pinkie toe found the edge of the coffee table. Before I could think, something flew out of my mouth. And I thought, ugh . . . that was honest.

Then there was the day I dropped my phone. Not a gentle slip, but one of those dramatic slow-motion tumbles where you watch it fall like it's your firstborn child diving off a cliff. Again—unfiltered words. Straight from the heart.

Worst of all was the near miss on the highway. One second I was humming along, the next second my heart was doing jumping jacks, and my adrenaline was trying to escape through my ears. What came out of my mouth in that moment? Let's just say it wasn't a hymn.

These unguarded moments are like tiny windows into what's really going on inside. They reveal the words that live in the basement of my heart, the ones that leap out before my Sunday self has time to tidy them up.

So I've been praying about it and paying much closer attention to what comes out of my mouth—not to muscle my tongue into obedience by sheer willpower, but to invite God to keep shaping me from the inside out through His powerful Word, just like this week's memory verse from Psalm 119 says.

Read Matthew 12:34c and Proverbs 4:23 in the margin. How might guarding your heart more closely change the way you speak and interact with others?

Out of the abundance of the heart the mouth speaks.

—Matthew 12:34c ESV

Guard your heart above all else, for it determines the course of your life.

—Proverbs 4:23

Now, let's return to Mephibosheth's story and read about *his* heart.

Read 2 Samuel 19:24 in the margin. Which three external expressions demonstrated his mourning?

1.

2.

3.

Now Mephibosheth, Saul's grandson, came down from Jerusalem to meet the king. He had not cared for his feet, trimmed his beard, or washed his clothes since the day the king left Jerusalem.

—2 Samuel 19:24

In an act of mourning, Mephibosheth had not cared for his feet, trimmed his beard, or washed his clothes since the day David left. In his culture, being unkempt was an outward sign of inward grief. His outward appearance revealed his inward anguish while the king was away.

Sheth truly grieved the loss of David, who had treated him like a son, and God knew the state of his heart.

When David returned, Sheth came down to welcome the brokenhearted king back to Jerusalem. Just as David had welcomed him as a younger man, now Sheth extended the same care and loyalty to David in his older years.

David had fled Jerusalem in the spring, likely in late April since this was harvest time. The days were warm. His exile lasted several weeks, stretching into summer—long enough for Absalom to seize Jerusalem, muster an army, and ultimately fall in battle. David's return was not immediate; it came only after the rebellion had collapsed.

Imagine how Sheth must have smelled that summer, having gone weeks without washing his clothes. His untrimmed beard left him looking scruffy and disheveled. Yet for someone with Sheth's disability, the most critical aspect of hygiene was proper care of his feet—a need that could not be neglected.

If Sheth was crippled due to neurological damage, as I suspect he may have been, he likely had no feeling in his feet. He wouldn't have felt a scrape or cut, allowing infection to go undetected without proper attention. In any case, as someone with a disability that affected mobility, caring for his feet was more important to his health than shaving or changing his clothes, which is one reason it is listed first. Still, when you're walking through bereavement, what once mattered easily slips into the background. Clearly, Sheth was deeply mourning the loss of the man who had been like a father to him.

If Mephibosheth had truly wanted Absalom to become king in place of David, it seems unlikely that he would have been openly grieving, neglecting his personal care and appearance. Beyond that, it would hardly have been wise for anyone hoping to gain Absalom's favor to present themself in such a neglected state, especially given how much Absalom valued outward appearance.

Scripture emphasizes his strikingly good looks, noting he was praised for his flawless appearance. Clearly, his image mattered greatly to him, and it is reasonable to assume he would have looked more favorably on those who reflected a similar concern.

Mephibosheth, however, seems to have valued matters of the heart over outward appearance—a reminder of what God values when looking for a king. We see this reflected in God's words to the prophet Samuel when selecting the king who replaced Sheth's grandfather, Saul.

But the Lord said to Samuel, "Do not look on his appearance or on the height of his stature, because I have rejected him. For the Lord sees not as man sees: man looks on the outward appearance, but the Lord looks on the heart."

—1 Samuel 16:7 ESV

Read 1 Samuel 16:7 in the margin and complete the columns below *based on your own experiences.*

What People Notice First	What God Notices First
____________________	____________________
____________________	____________________
____________________	____________________

Samuel anointed David, a man after God's own heart. Though deeply flawed, David was also deeply loved. We, too, are broken, and yet we are beloved. Nothing we have done earns God's love, and nothing we do can make Him stop loving us. David's life stands as a testimony to the depths to which we can fall. Yet just as David turned to God in honest contrition, we, too, can pray the same prayer of repentance.

Look up Psalm 51:10 (ESV) and fill in the blanks of David's prayer:

Create in me a clean ____________, *O God,*

and renew a right ________ *within me.*

For me, this verse has become a simple prayer I often match with my breathing. As I inhale, I pray, "Create in me a clean heart." And as I exhale, I pray, "and renew a right spirit within me." Praying this prayer helps my spirit to align with the Holy Spirit's calming presence and peace. While I certainly haven't arrived, I am moving in the right direction. You are too!

I applaud you for drawing close to God over these weeks of our study. You have been faithful to hide His Word in your heart. He is purifying and renewing your spirit as you read and study. Keep pressing on, remembering that God cares more about your heart than anything external, because it determines the course of your life!

Enter into a time of worship. Scan this QR code to listen to "Hard Fought Hallelujah" by Brandon Lake.

Reread this week's memory verse and fill in the blank.

I have hidden your __________ in my heart,
that I might not sin against you.
I praise you, O LORD;
teach me your decrees.
—Psalm 119:11-12

Write your name in the blank and let this become the blessing Jesus whispers over your heart.

My Beloved________________, others may judge by what they see, but I see your heart attitude—the quiet yes, the hidden surrender, the courage no one else notices. When betrayal stings and the path feels lonely, know this: I am nearer than breath. I hold every tear, strengthen every step, and rejoice over every small act of faithfulness. Rest in My delight. You are My cherished daughter, and I will never let you go.

Now offer your response: *Jesus, . . .*

Day 3: Stay Faithful to the King

Biblical Foundation:
Psalm 145:9; James 3:13-16; Romans 12:15

Focus Scripture:
"Why didn't you come with me, Mephibosheth?" the king asked him.

Mephibosheth replied, "My lord the king, my servant Ziba deceived me. I told him, 'Saddle my donkey so I can go with the king.' For as you know I am crippled. Ziba has slandered me by saying that I refused to come."

—2 Samuel 19:25-27a

Today we'll discover that Mephibosheth was a true friend to David—one who was faithful in both sorrow and celebration. He mourned when the king mourned, and he rejoiced when David returned to Jerusalem. We all need friends like Sheth: faithful companions who remain steady when life rises and falls.

Years earlier David also had a true friend in Sheth's dad, Jonathan. Jonathan's name in Hebrew means "Yahweh has given,"[5] reminding us that every good gift in our lives begins with God's generous heart. The same God who gave Jonathan as a blessing to David, and later gave Sheth as a blessing to David, continues to give us the gift of friendship today.

My prayer for you and the other women in your group is that your friendships will deepen and you will experience the kind of loyal, God-given companionship David knew.

We'll see how Mephibosheth remained faithful to David even when others fell away. Sheth chose loyalty over self-protection and self-promotion. His example invites us to trust God with our reputation, do what is right, and walk in faithfulness.

Reread today's Focus Scripture, 2 Samuel 19:25-27a above. How would you restate Mephibosheth's final comment in your own words?

For many reasons, most commentators agree that Ziba was indeed slandering Mephibosheth. He appeared at the very moment David was heartbroken and fleeing, arriving with baskets of supplies and a perfectly polished tale about Sheth's supposed betrayal. Commentators point out that Ziba's timing suggests he knew David was vulnerable and ready to believe the worst. And of course, Ziba had the most to gain. We saw in Day 1 that the moment he finished talking, David gave him all of Sheth's land. That instant reward makes his motives appear more opportunistic than loyal.

Sheth's appearance upon David's return, however, tells a completely different story. We learned yesterday that Sheth hadn't cared for his feet, trimmed his beard, or washed his clothes the entire time David was gone. Commentators note how his grief and loyalty bear witness to his genuine heart, especially since he had always shown deep humility and gratitude toward David. His explanation—that Ziba abandoned him and twisted the truth—fits the character Scripture has already shown us of Ziba.

Ziba's motive, timing, and personal gain along with Sheth's consistent character all point to the same probable conclusion: Ziba lied. The story serves as a gentle reminder for anyone who has ever been misjudged or betrayed: People may jump to conclusions, but God sees the heart, the truth, and the quiet faithfulness others miss.

Share a time when you were slandered. Did someone take credit for your gifts or work, as happened to Sheth? What motives do you think may have been behind their actions?

Though we cannot say for certain, I believe Ziba may have lied because he resented serving Sheth. Ziba once served royalty, which likely elevated his status. Then David assigned him to serve Sheth's household. Suddenly, Sheth was wealthier than Ziba was after years of service to the king. I believe Ziba may have been envious of Sheth, whom he likely felt did nothing to deserve David's generosity.

Read James 3:13-16 below and circle every negative attitude.

If you are wise and understand God's ways, prove it by living an honorable life, doing good works with the humility that comes from wisdom. But if you are bitterly jealous and there is selfish ambition in your heart, don't cover up the truth with boasting and lying. For jealousy and selfishness are not God's kind of wisdom. Such things are earthly, unspiritual, and demonic. For wherever there is jealousy and selfish ambition, there you will find disorder and evil of every kind.

—James 3:13-16

Where have you seen disorder or tension in your life that might be caused by jealousy or selfish ambition?

How have you responded to that tension, and what has it produced in you or in others?

Ziba was likely driven by jealousy and selfish ambitions. Perhaps he perceived his new assignment of serving a man who ordinarily would be looked down upon in their day as a demotion. It was likely greed and a combination of many negative emotions that motivated Ziba's actions.

Recently I've learned two German words that describe two emotions at opposite ends of the spectrum. *Schadenfreude* is built from the German words *Schaden* (harm) and *Freude* (joy), a compact expression for a feeling English can describe but not match with a single word. It lurks in the same emotional neighborhood as Ziba's envy, though it expresses itself differently.

Schadenfreude is the dark delight in another's misfortune—perhaps felt by Ziba after he slandered Sheth. It's the twisted comfort that whispers, "If you lose something, I feel better about myself." This impulse grows in hearts convinced that God's blessings are limited—that someone else's rise threatens our own security. In Ziba's case, it seems that the temptation toward *Schadenfreude* fueled manipulation and deceit, revealing how envy can curdle into a desire to see another diminished.

Schadenfreude shrinks the soul, turning us away from God's expansive love. It warns us that when we cannot celebrate another's gain, we may soon find ourselves secretly hoping for their loss. But God doesn't work this way. His kingdom isn't a win-lose arena where one person's rise requires another's fall. In God's economy, grace multiplies; it's never rationed. Everyone can flourish. Scripture consistently reflects God's generous love and wide-open compassion, where another's blessing is not a threat but an invitation to trust the King who has more seats at His table.

The LORD is good to everyone.
He showers compassion
on all his creation.
—Psalm 145:9

Read Psalm 145:9 in the margin. Place a check mark next to each person who receives God's compassion.

____ those who are compassionate to others
____ those who are righteous
____ those who slander us
____ those who take credit for our gifts

All means those we consider "good" and those we consider "bad" and everyone in between.

On the opposite side of the canyon of *Schadenfreude* is *Freudenfreude. Freudenfreude* is the joy we feel in response to another person's blessing—the emotional opposite of Ziba's reaction to Sheth's restoration. *Freudenfreude* comes from the German words *Freude* (joy) and *freuen* (to rejoice), forming a term that English doesn't have a sufficient single-word equivalent for.

Freudenfreude requires a heart spacious enough to applaud someone else's elevation even when it highlights our own lack—a willingness to say, "Your gain does not diminish me." It's a spiritual discipline that loosens envy's grip and frees us to participate in God's generosity.

Jonathan's words and actions show that he felt *Freudenfreude* toward David, rejoicing in his victories and his anointing as the next king. He celebrated David's rise even though it meant he himself would never ascend to his father's throne.

Had Ziba embraced *Freudenfreude,* Sheth's seat at the royal table could have become a shared celebration of God's mercy rather than a threat that fueled his own ambitions. *Freudenfreude* invites us to rejoice when God lifts another, trusting that His goodness is abundant rather than scarce—and that someone else's blessing is never the limit of our own.

When have you experienced *Freudenfreude*—feeling happy for another person's gain?

Read Romans 12:15 in the margin. Then respond as honestly as you can to each question using a scale from 1 (easy) to 5 (hard):

How easy is it for you to rejoice with others?

1-------------2------------3------------4------------5

How easy is it for you to weep with others?

1-------------2------------3------------4------------5

> Be happy with those who are happy, and weep with those who weep.
>
> ***—Romans 12:15***

We all need friends like Sheth—those who rejoice when we rejoice and lift us up when we are beaten down. Prayerfully consider this today: Who are those friends in your life? And to whom are you that kind of faithful friend?

Enter into a time of worship. Scan this QR code to listen to "Thank God I Do" by Lauren Daigle.

Reread this week's memory verse and fill in the blanks.

I have hidden your_________ in my heart,
that I might not ________ against you.
I praise you, O LORD;
teach me your decrees.
—Psalm 119:11-12

Write your name in the blank and let this become the blessing Jesus whispers over your heart.

Beloved________________, I delight in the heart that seeks Me above all else. When you are misunderstood or slandered, rest in Me. I know every wound, and I am your defender and healer. Let Me mature you so you can rejoice with those who rejoice and weep with those who weep. Let Me shape your heart so that you never gloat over another's pain but long for every person to rise. My love is infinite and overflowing. There is enough to lift you and everyone around you.

Now offer your response: *Jesus, . . .*

Day 4: Be Grateful for the King

Biblical Foundations:
2 Samuel 19:27b-28; Psalm 51:12; Luke 15:11-28, 31-32

Focus Scripture:
"But I know that my lord the king is like an angel of God, so do what you think is best. All my relatives and I could expect only death from you, my lord, but instead you have honored me by allowing me to eat at your own table! What more can I ask?"
—2 Samuel 19:27b-28

When good things happen to you, do you think you deserve them? My hardworking dad felt he earned good by the sweat of his brow. But my mom had a different perspective. She saw life through the eyes of faith and taught me to be grateful for everything, knowing that every good gift points us to the Good Gift Giver.

Science has proven that the spiritual discipline of gratefulness has huge implications on our mental and physical health. Gratitude is one of the most powerful practices, and its impact shows up in our appreciation of everyday moments—a quiet cup of coffee, a child's hug, a friend's well-timed text.

Research shows that gratitude activates brain regions linked to joy, bonding, and resilience, helping us handle stress. Studies have also found that gratitude lowers symptoms of anxiety and depression and increases overall life satisfaction.[6]

Physically, gratitude is associated with better sleep, lower inflammation, and healthier hearts. And relationally, expressing gratitude strengthens trust and empathy, creating the kind of connection that helps families and friendships flourish.[7] Gratitude isn't just a feeling—it's a God-designed practice that strengthens mind, body, and relationships.

All this information reminds me that our Creator knows us inside and out. He understands every beat of what makes our hearts happy. Now let's turn to Sheth's personal story of gratitude.

"All my relatives and I could expect only death from you, my lord, but instead you have honored me by allowing me to eat at your own table! What more can I ask?"

—2 Samuel 19:28

Read 2 Samuel 19:28 in the margin. How do Sheth's words reveal his attitude of gratitude?

Mephibosheth's words reveal a heart anchored not in entitlement but in deep gratitude. Though wronged and vulnerable, he places himself fully in David's hands, releasing any demand for more and gratefully resting in the grace he has been given.

This brings to mind another man in Scripture—one tucked inside what is often called the parable of the prodigal son. Today, though, I'd like us to look at this familiar story through a different lens, renaming it the parable of the faithful son and viewing it through the lens of gratitude.

Turn to Luke 15 and hold your place there. Read verses 11-25. Who stands out to you in this parable?

When hearing this story, many people immediately connect with the prodigal son who wandered, failed, and finally came home. But commentators remind us that the older son is just as important, representing a different kind of lostness—the kind that hides behind responsibility and faithfulness. Many of us know this feeling well. It's the quiet ache of being the dependable one who rarely gets celebrated because she rarely falls apart. When someone else who has made a mess receives positive attention or compassion, it can stir up emotions we don't like to admit.

This is when *Schadenfreude*—that subtle satisfaction we feel when someone else stumbles—which we learned about yesterday, can creep in. We tend to feel it not because we're cruel but because we're feeling tired or unseen.

Now read Luke 15:25-28 and list below the emotions you detect in these verses.

I imagine the elder son trudging in from the fields. He was probably sweaty and smelly, with an attitude that wasn't much fresher. Though anger is mentioned in verse 28, I also detect possible surprise and resentment. He had faithfully worked for his father, being a dutiful son; but his younger brother, who had irresponsibly asked for his inheritance and left to live as he pleased, was being thrown a welcome-home party. Surely the older son must have felt he was the one who was entitled to such an extravagant celebration. Into this emotional landscape, the story of Mephibosheth shines like a healing light.

Sheth had not rebelled as the younger son had, yet he was deeply grateful for grace when David welcomed him to the royal table. He knew he had nothing to offer. His gratitude shows us what it looks like to receive love without entitlement, a posture the older son struggled to embrace. Mephibosheth offers us a living picture of the heart God wants to form in us: a heart that knows we are loved and rejoices when others are lifted up.

Many commentators point out that the older son symbolizes the Pharisees—those who resented God's mercy toward messy people. In Sheth's story, Ziba plays a similar role—resenting David's compassionate treatment of the crippled son of the former king. We learned yesterday that Ziba likely slandered Sheth, misrepresenting him. Ziba embodies the mindset that "there's not enough grace to go around." The older son embodies the mindset that "I earned my place; he didn't." Both attitudes choke out *Freudenfreude*—the ability to rejoice when someone else is lifted up.

As women, we often feel this tension in friendships, ministry teams, or family dynamics. When someone who hurt us or disappointed us is restored, our inner Ziba-voice whispers, "They don't deserve it." Jesus exposes this inner posture in the parable not to shame us but to free us.

The older son's jealousy is painfully human. He sees the party thrown for his brother and feels invisible. Perhaps you've known this ache—when a friend gets the promotion, the engagement, the baby, the recognition, or the breakthrough you've prayed for. This is when God invites us into *Freudenfreude*—the joy of celebrating someone else's joy. It's a spiritual maturity that doesn't come naturally but grows with the help of the Holy Spirit as we rest in God's love.

Mephibosheth models *Freudenfreude* beautifully. When Ziba tries to steal his inheritance and slander him, Sheth doesn't respond with bitterness or *Schadenfreude.* Instead, he shares how grateful he is that David has accepted him at all. His heart is free from *Schadenfreude* because he knows he is loved. His posture shows us how to live unthreatened by others' blessings. When we know we have a seat at the King's table, we don't panic when someone else is invited.

While the younger prodigal son was lost in *defiance,* the older faithful son was lost in *duty*. He stayed home, but his heart wandered. Many of us can relate to this; we serve faithfully in church and care for family, yet we feel distant from God's joy. When we live in *duty* instead of *delight,* *Schadenfreude* becomes more tempting because our hearts feel empty. We begin to think, "I deserve something for all I've done."

The older son's resentment reveals a heart that has forgotten intimacy and lost gratitude. Sheth again offers a contrast. He had every reason to feel overlooked—disabled, displaced, forgotten—yet when grace found him, he responded with humility and gratitude. He shows us how to receive love without resentment and stay tender even when life has been harsh.

When we know we have a seat at the King's table, we don't panic when someone else is invited.

Restore to me the joy of your salvation,
and make me willing to obey you.

—Psalm 51:12

Read Psalm 51:12 in the margin and paraphrase it below as a personal prayer to God.

I pray this often as a breath prayer when my joy seems to be lost through the sieve of daily responsibilities. We all have times when we feel the struggle of the older son, who said, "All these years I've slaved for you" (Luke 15:29).

When have you felt you were doing everything for everyone but were unappreciated?

When we serve from exhaustion instead of intimacy, we are more likely to lose the ability to be grateful and celebrate others. *Freudenfreude* requires a full heart; *Schadenfreude* grows in a depleted one. Mephibosheth's story reminds us that *identity* comes before *activity*. He sat at the king's table before he ever "did" anything for the king. We need this reminder to serve *from love*, not *for love*, trusting there's an unending supply of God's love.

Let's return to the parable of the faithful son once more.

Read Luke 15:28-32. What stands out to you in these verses?

Commentators emphasize that the father goes out to talk with the older son, just as he ran out to the younger one. He not only goes out to him; he *begs* him to join the party. This is stunning! God pursues both the *rebellious* and the *resentful*. For those of us who feel overlooked, tired, or hardened by years of quiet faithfulness, this is hope.

The father doesn't scold; he invites.

He doesn't shun; he embraces.

Jesus leaves the ending of the parable open so that each of us can decide whether we will stay stuck in *Schadenfreude* (like Ziba and the older son) or step into the joy of *Freudenfreude* (like Sheth and the father in this parable). Mephibosheth's gratitude stands in beautiful contrast to the older son's entitlement. The parable invites us to become like Sheth—to sit at the King's table with humble, joyful, grateful hearts, knowing every gift is grace.

May you take your place at the King's table with open hands and a grateful heart, rejoicing that everything before you is a gift of grace. Our King wants us to enjoy our gifts. He wants to sustain us. He wants us to look to Him for all our needs!

Enter into a time of worship. Scan this QR code to listen to "Jesus Loves" by Zach Williams.

Reread this week's memory verse and fill in the blanks.

I have hidden your ____________ in my heart,
that I might not __________ against you.
I ____________ you, O Lord;
teach me your decrees.
—Psalm 119:11-12

Write your name in the blank and let this become the blessing Jesus whispers over your heart.

Beloved ________________, come close to Me. I never ask you to serve Me out of duty, but only out of the delight that grows when you rest in my love. Serve not for love, but from love. Rejoice when others receive grace, just as heaven rejoices over the returning child. And know this: I see every unseen act of faithfulness. You are My forever-faithful daughter, and I treasure you.

Now offer your response: *Jesus, . . .*

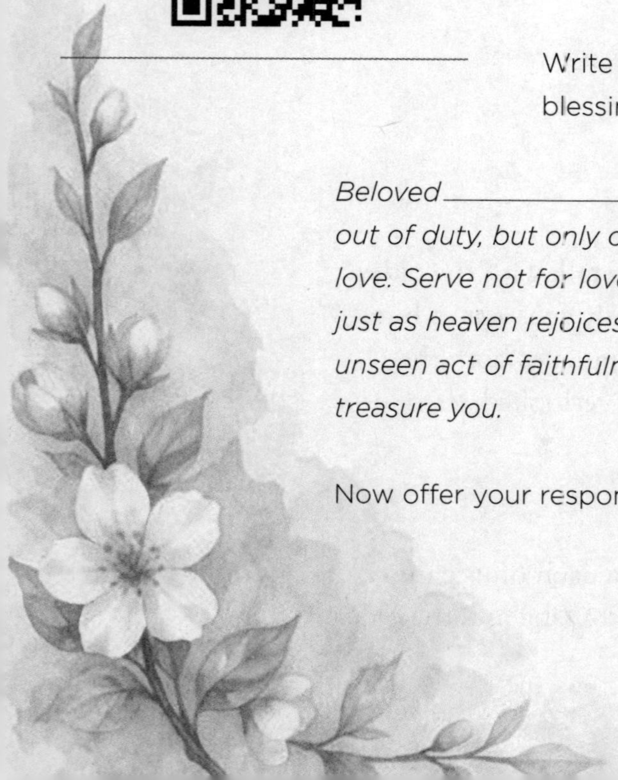

Day 5: Be Content with the King

Biblical Foundations:
2 Samuel 19:29-30; Ecclesiastes 5:10; Luke 18:18-23; 1 Timothy 6:7-8; Hebrews 13:5

Focus Scripture:
"You've said enough," David replied. "I've decided that you and Ziba will divide your land equally between you."

"Give him all of it," Mephibosheth said. "I am content just to have you safely back again, my lord the king!"
—2 Samuel 19:29-30

Today is our final lesson in a week that started with chaotic battles and betrayals. Throughout these days we have learned the importance of guarding our hearts so we remain faithful even when others fall away. We discovered that true service flows not from *duty* but from *delight*; serving *from* love, not *for* love.

Yesterday we explored the transforming power of gratitude. Life is challenging, yet even in difficulty we can experience radiant joy. Gratitude can reshape our attitude, as we saw in the parable of the prodigal son.

Today we'll be blessed with another truth that few of us ever *fully* experience: the joy of contentment—contentment *in* and *with* what the King provides. Before *possessions* have a chance to *possess* us, the King invites us into a better way. We'll see this clearly through Jesus's encounter with the rich man in Luke 18. The story is recorded in all three Synoptic Gospels because its message is vital.

Turn to Luke 18 and put a placeholder there. Read verses 18-19. What does the man's question reveal about his heart?

How does Jesus's response expose the deeper issue?

> Someone came to Jesus with this question: "Teacher, what good deed must I do to have eternal life?"
>
> —***Matthew 19:16***

Luke's Gospel tells us that the rich man calls Jesus "Good Teacher" (Luke 18:18)—a respectful title that subtly keeps Jesus at a safe distance—and then asks what he must do to inherit eternal life. In Matthew's Gospel, we read that the man asks "what good deed" he must do (see the margin). It's clear he believes eternal life is something earned; a spiritual task to complete. His assumption seems to be that eternal life is a reward for moral achievement. His heart seems to be sincere but self-reliant.

With his response, Jesus gently unsettles that framework and challenges the man's understanding of goodness, shifting the focus from *what* goodness is to *who* goodness is. It is an invitation to think more deeply about who God is and what true goodness means.

Jesus then points him to the commandments.

Read Luke 18:20-21. What commandments does Jesus name here?

Luke lists the core relational commandments: Do not commit adultery, do not murder, do not steal, do not lie, and honor your parents. Matthew adds "love your neighbor as yourself" (19:19), and Mark adds "do not defraud" (10:19 ESV). The man sincerely replies that he has kept these since his youth. Jesus does not correct him. His obedience and discipline seem to be genuine, but Jesus is preparing him to see that rule-keeping alone cannot give life. Something deeper is needed; something that touches the *heart*, not just the *habits*. Then Jesus moves to the center of the man's struggle.

Read Luke 18:22-24. Paraphrase what Jesus told him to do. Why do you think Jesus told him to do this?

Luke highlights the man's extreme wealth. Mark includes a tender detail that shows us the heart of Jesus: "Jesus looked at him and loved him" (10:21 NIV). Matthew emphasizes the call to wholeness: "If you want to be perfect..." (19:21).

Jesus lovingly exposes the one thing the man cannot release. He invites him to sell his possessions, give to the poor, and follow Him. This is not about *money*; it is about *surrender*. Jesus is not trying to take something away. He is inviting the man into freedom: treasure in heaven and a life built on following Him.

The man's response is heartbreaking. Luke says he became very sad because "he was extremely rich" (18:23 ESV). Matthew says, "He went away sorrowful" (19:22 ESV). Mark says his "face fell" (10:22). His sadness reveals the truth: He wanted *salvation*, but he didn't want to *surrender*. He wanted to add Jesus to his life, not rebuild his life around Jesus. His wealth wasn't just something he owned; it was something that owned him. This is one of the few Gospel stories where someone walks away from Jesus. This is the only time Jesus tells anyone to sell all they have and give the money to the poor.

When we look at all three Gospels together, we see a man who is moral, sincere, and spiritually interested—and deeply loved by Jesus. His obstacle is not wickedness but unhealthy attachment. The issue is not wealth itself but what wealth can do to the heart. His story invites us to examine our own hearts.

The rich ruler is not a villain—he is a mirror. Jesus wasn't trying to diminish the man's life. He was offering him a better one. The same invitation is open to us: not to earn eternal life but to follow the One who gives it. Jesus calls us away from whatever *holds our hearts* so He can *fill our hands* with something better!

Jesus calls us away from whatever *holds our hearts* so He can *fill our hands* with something better!

The rich man's struggle to surrender his heart to Jesus reminds me of two images my pastor once shared—similar to the ones below—along with a piercing question:

Which tent do you live in: disconTENTment or conTENTment? Circle the tent you're living in right now.

Keep your lives free from the love of money and be content with what you have, because God has said,
"Never will I leave you;
never will I forsake you."
—Hebrews 13:5 NIV

Read Hebrews 13:5 in the margin. Underline the word *love* and circle the word *content*.

Money itself is not evil; it's morally neutral. It's the love of money—greed, craving, and misplaced trust—that can lead to all kinds of trouble. The warning in this passage speaks to the heart, not the wallet.

Now, let's return to Mephibosheth's story with our hearts open to hear the gratitude that flows from his heart.

Reread 2 Samuel 19:27-28 in the margin. Underline the words or phrases that convey Sheth's gratitude.

"But I know that my lord the king is like an angel of God, so do what you think is best. All my relatives and I could expect only death from you, my lord, but instead you have honored me by allowing me to eat at your own table! What more can I ask?"

—2 Samuel 19:27-28

Sheth was grateful for all he had been given and humbly deferred to King David's judgment. He was overwhelmed with thanksgiving as he cherished the honor of being allowed to eat at the king's table.

Now read 2 Samuel 19:29-30 in the margin, and paraphrase King David's response in your own words.

"You've said enough," David replied. "I've decided that you and Ziba will divide your land equally between you."

"Give him all of it," Mephibosheth said. "I am content just to have you safely back again, my lord the king!"

—2 Samuel 19:29-30

What does Mephibosheth's reply reveal about what he values most of all—and what makes him content?

Seeing Sheth's heart humbles me and makes me ponder: *Would I honestly respond as he did if I were in his place?* My first instinct would be to think, *This isn't fair.* Sheth lost half of his property. But that isn't where Sheth's eyes were fixed. He cared nothing about the *things* and everything about the *one* he loved, David.

Sheth knew that he and his relatives deserved nothing; if anything, they could expect only death. Instead, they were given life and a seat at the King's table. His story is a picture of the grace we've received. We, too, could expect death, yet we have been given abundant life along with an invitation to become children of God.

No doubt Sheth remembered, with a grateful heart, the years he had spent lonely, shamed, and forgotten in the house of a man named *bartered*, living in a land of no-thing. That memory surely shaped his heart of gratitude.

On this continuum of surrender, the Rich Man stands on the left and Sheth on the right. Circle where you find yourself in this season.

1 2 3 4 5 6 7 8 9 10

Whoever loves money never has enough;
whoever loves wealth is never satisfied with their income.
—Ecclesiastes 5:10 (NIV)

For we brought nothing into the world, and we can take nothing out of it. But if we have food and clothing, we will be content with that.
—1 Timothy 6:7-8 (NIV)

Know that wherever you find yourself today, there is no shame but only your King calling you closer. May gratitude soften your grip on whatever you're holding and lead you, with open hands and a willing heart, to take your place at His table.

Reread this week's memory verse and fill in the blanks.

I have hidden your __________ in my heart,

that I might not ________ against you.

I __________ you, O Lord;

teach me your decrees.

—Psalm 119:11-12

Write your name in the blank and let this become the blessing Jesus whispers over your heart.

My beloved ______________, thank you for coming to Me with a heart that simply wants My presence. I cherish every moment you choose to sit with Me. Your nearness brings Me joy. I love giving you gifts that no earthly treasure can match—love, joy, peace, patience, kindness, goodness, faithfulness, gentleness, and self-control.

Now offer your response: *Jesus, . . .*

Enter into a time of worship. Scan this QR code to listen to "Holy Forever" by Chris Tomlin.

Week 5

Video Viewer Guide

1. Some friends are ______________, but a true friend stands by you like ____________________.

2. True friendship fosters ________________, not ________________.

3. A true friend doesn't just ________________ but points you back to __________.

4. A true friend ___________________________ you when others _____________________________________ you.

5. A true friend loves you enough to tell you the ____________________.

6. A true friendship is never about what we ______________ but about what we ______________.

What pieces of the pie will you entrust to God: your family, finances, friendships, identity, dreams, and decisions? If your heart were a pie chart, which slices have you truly entrusted to Jesus, our King? Shade those portions as a quiet prayer of surrender.

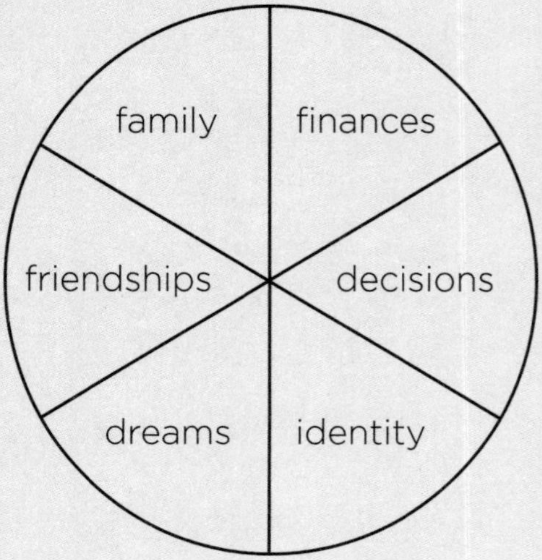

WEEK 6

Experiencing Perfect Love

Memory Verse

"I will teach all your children,
and they will enjoy great peace."

—Isaiah 54:13

Recipe of the Week

Here is my Loaded Potato Soup recipe. I thicken the roux with potato flakes instead of flour, which makes it gluten-free. Of all the foods in my pantry, these flakes look the most like manna, described in Exodus 16:14 and 31 as a white, flaky substance. This week we'll talk about manna and God's invitation to come to Him daily!

Recipe

Gluten-Free Loaded Potato Soup

INGREDIENTS

- 4 tbsp. butter
- 1 medium onion, diced
- 2 cloves garlic, minced
- 4 cups chicken broth (You can substitute bouillon powder.)
- 4 cups russet potatoes, skinned and cut in chunks
- 2 cups half-and-half or milk
- 1-1½ cups potato flakes
- Salt and pepper to taste
- *Optional* toppings: shredded cheddar, bacon, green onion, sour cream

DIRECTIONS

1. Melt butter; then caramelize onions and garlic in a heavy pot to prevent scorching.
2. Add broth and potatoes. Simmer potatoes 15 minutes until fork-tender.
3. Pour in half-and-half or milk. Warm, don't boil, to prevent scorching.
4. Thicken by slowly adding potato flakes, stirring constantly to reach your preferred thickness.
5. Season to taste with salt, pepper, and toppings.

Note: Soup will thicken as it cools.

Introduction to This Week

Isaiah 54:13

Over the past five weeks, we've witnessed God's love shine on Mephibosheth through David. As I've shared previously, the first thing I see when I look at **Me**phibosheth is **me**. I hope you see yourself too. His story can be our story. If you've ever felt left out and have longed for an invitation, my prayer is that His grace-filled story has shown you God's love and a forever invitation to His table.

Like Mephibosheth, we've all been dropped—by someone, somewhere, at some time. And just as he survived a fall, we, too, have survived our falls. Though we are fallen people with imperfect families who worship in imperfect churches and live in an imperfect world, we are perfectly loved—because we are God's beloved children. This will be our focus this week.

Our King of kings longs to fill our souls with every good thing and to give us rest, a new name, a new purpose, and a lasting legacy. Like Mephibosheth, He invites us to come out of hiding from low places so He can lift us high and exchange our cloaks of shame for robes of righteousness. We are invited to the King's table, where grace covers our brokenness just as it covered Sheth's.

Day 1: Come Every Day

Biblical Foundations:
Exodus 16:14-15, 21; Deuteronomy 8:2-3; Matthew 22:1-14

Focus Scripture:
"*Remember how the* L*ORD your God led you through the wilderness for these forty years, humbling you and testing you to prove your character, and to find out whether or not you would obey his commands. Yes, he humbled you by letting you go hungry and then feeding you with manna, a food previously unknown to you and your ancestors.* ***He did it to teach you that people do not live by bread alone; rather, we live by every word that comes from the mouth of the Lord.***"
—Deuteronomy 8:2-3 (*emphasis added*)

As we've learned in earlier weeks of our study, Sheth lived close to the king so he could eat continually at his table. This simple detail invites a deeper question: Will we choose to stay close to our King so we can be fed by Him continually? He invites us to dine with Him every day, coming whenever our hearts hunger for love, acceptance, peace, and understanding.

You, my friend, have shown a desire for more of Him. Throughout these weeks, you have faithfully come to the table, reaching for the meat of God's Word rather than the empty calories of the world. This brings us to this crucial question: Will we continue to crave the "meat" that truly sustains us—the spiritual nourishment that goes far beyond the ordinary?

We've learned that in ancient times, meat was a luxury beyond the reach of ordinary families, while bread was the daily staple that bound households together. Sheth likely didn't eat meat regularly until he sat at the king's table—and what a table it must have been: King David surrounded by his many sons, loyal warriors, trusted advisors, and honored guests.

Regardless of how many gather around our own tables, the table is a symbol of community, provision, and belonging—a place where relationships are nurtured, generosity is shared, and God's abundant care is made tangible.

Who sits at your table on a regular basis? How often do you gather around the table—not just to eat, but to connect? What joy rises in you when the seats at your table are full?

I imagine David felt a similar joy when he saw how faithfully Sheth and his other family members came to his table in gratitude. Sheth recognized his need for companionship with the king, and he honored the invitation with his presence. Do we honor our King's invitation with that same joyful presence, or do we come begrudgingly, seeing the invitation as more of a duty or interruption than a gift?

As the Book of Exodus recounts, God's people often missed His invitation to depend on Him through the food provided in the wilderness, forgetting that each meal was a sign of His nearness and His willingness to provide. You may remember that God sent manna for them to eat. This "bread from heaven" provided sustenance, pointing them daily to Him, their Sustainer. Let's read about their first impression of manna.

Read Exodus 16:14-21, 31. Picture yourself stepping out to gather manna. Are you laughing with the women beside you, grateful for this daily miracle? Or are you half-awake and quietly grumbling, trying to imagine one more way to prepare the same heavenly provision?

The Hebrew word for manna is *mān*, and it literally means "What is it?" I'm a bit hesitant to try new foods. Of all the items in my pantry, I imagine manna to most closely resemble our modern-day potato flakes, which is why I chose *Loaded Potato Soup* for this week's recipe.

Read Numbers 11:8 in the margin. How does it say they prepared the manna?

> The people would go out and gather it from the ground. They made flour by grinding it with hand mills or pounding it in mortars. Then they boiled it in a pot and made it into flat cakes. These cakes tasted like pastries baked with olive oil.
>
> ***—Numbers 11:8***

Don't you know the Israelite women shared many creative ways to prepare the manna—much as we do with basic ingredients. I imagine them roasting it, baking it into breads and cakes, and boiling it for soups. I'm sure they came up with some wonderful recipes, even if they longed for more seasoning like the garlic, onions, and leeks they wistfully remembered from Egypt (Numbers 11:5). But unlike you and me, the women had to "shop" for ingredients first thing every morning.

God invited His people to form a loving habit—beginning each morning with gratitude and trust in His care. The manna "melted" as the sun grew hot. What a tender picture for us. We can come to God daily to receive the encouragement our hearts need so we don't *melt* under the fiery trials the day may bring.

If your schedule doesn't allow you to come early, our King understands. For the many years I worked full-time as a pharmacist while raising children, it was a struggle to spend time relaxing in God's presence when so many responsibilities screamed for my attention. Sheth likely came to the king's table later in the day, yet the beauty is this: he came. The same is true for us. What matters most is not the hour on the clock but the posture of our hearts. He delights in every moment we come.

Look up Deuteronomy 8:2-3. Then insert the missing words below into the crossword puzzle as directed.

Yes, [God] humbled you by letting you go hungry and then feeding you with manna, a food previously unknown to you and your ancestors. He did it to teach you that people do not (1 across) by (1 down) alone; rather, we live by every (2 across) that comes from the mouth of the Lord.

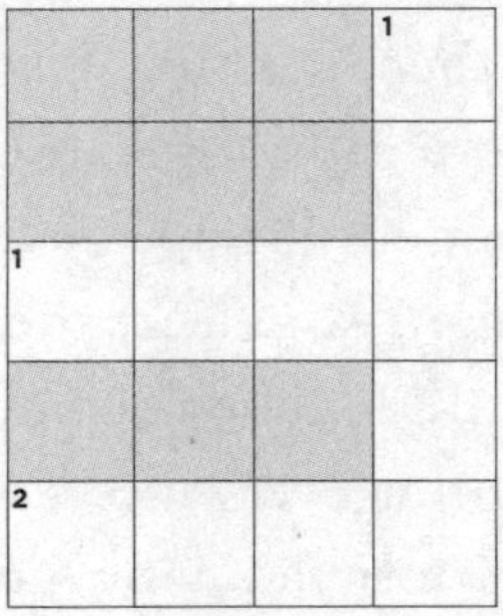

As I write, buttery garlic bread is baking in my oven, along with homemade cheesy lasagna. In just a few hours, our son Garrett, his fiancée, and her parents will arrive. They are in town for the wedding of their daughter and our son later this week. My heart is full, overjoyed that Garrett has found a wonderful Christian woman to be his bride.

As I set the dining room table with china—something I reserve only for special occasions—my thoughts drifted to another table. Though our King's table will be far longer and grander than mine, I imagine it will feel wonderfully special and personal. Let's read about it in the parable of the king's wedding banquet.

Read Matthew 22:1-14. Who in the parable do you most resemble?

Jesus revealed the heart of His Father when He told the parable of the king's wedding banquet. The king prepares a joyful celebration and invites *everyone*, yet many ignore Him or offer excuses. Still, His invitation keeps expanding—reaching the overlooked, the busy, the broken, and the unlikely.

The wedding garments remind us that we don't enter by our own goodness but by receiving the grace He provides through Christ. To refuse His invitation is to minimize His gift of grace. Our King isn't looking for *perfection*; He's looking for *presence*, for a willing heart that says yes to His love. His final call is tender and urgent. Many are invited, but few are chosen.

You are invited and chosen!

Like Sheth, do you believe our King's invitation is heartfelt, and how will you respond?

This week's memory verse is dear to my heart. It's the promise my mom prayed over me every morning and evening as she traced the sign of the cross with her thumb on my forehead and on the foreheads of my siblings. She made the verse her own prayer, proclaiming,

---

You are a child of God,
taught of the Lord,
great will be your peace and undisturbed composure.

Like my mom, I bless my children and grandchildren with this verse every time I greet them and say goodbye. My three-year-old grandson has come to expect it, rushing to be first in line. Though he doesn't understand the full implications, he knows this blessing is something good. He makes sure everyone in his family is blessed before they leave.

We didn't have much when I was growing up. My family of five lived in a one-bedroom house until my dad built a second bedroom on the back. In the world's eyes, we were poor, but we were rich in love. I didn't know what my future held, but I knew who held my future. My King loved me then, and He loves me now. He loves you too! He wants to provide for your needs. He wants you to know you can count on Him. He enjoys your company and longs for you to come to Him so that He can bless you and shower you with His love.

Enter into a time of worship. Scan this QR code to listen to "Come Jesus Come" by CeCe Winans.

Reread this week's memory verse.

> *"I will teach all your children,*
> *and they will enjoy great peace."*
> —Isaiah 54:13

Write your name in the blank and let this become the blessing Jesus whispers over your heart.

My beloved _______________, come to My table as you are, and come often to receive what your soul truly needs. I delight when you draw near. Rest in My presence and breathe in My joy. And as you look toward the day when all My children gather at My heavenly table, hold this truth close: you are Mine, taught by Me, and great will be your peace.

Now offer your response: *Jesus, . . .*

Day 2: Your New Name

Biblical Foundations:
Exodus 3:13-14; Isaiah 43:13; 49:15-16a; Galatians 4:6; Revelation 2:17b-c

Focus Scripture:
"To everyone who is victorious I will give some of the manna that has been hidden away in heaven. And I will give to each one a white stone, and on the stone will be engraved a new name that no one understands except the one who receives it."
—Revelation 2:17b-c

From 1982 to 1993, viewers tuned into the award-winning sitcom *Cheers*. While I don't remember all the characters, I do remember the tagline and tune from the theme song "Where Everybody Knows Your Name." It was such a huge hit for so long because we all want to be invited to a place "where everybody knows your name, and they're always glad you came."

While everyone knows me as Lisa, my given name is Elizabeth—or "Elisabet" in Greek, the language of the New Testament. For me, it's comforting to see "Lisa" nestled in the middle because people have always looked at me funny when they learn that I'm an Elizabeth who goes by Lisa.

On my first day of kindergarten, I still remember my teacher taking roll and pointing students toward the desks with their names on them. I had practiced how to print "L-I-S-A." My eyes scanned the room, but I couldn't find a desk with those letters. Since I didn't know my name was Elizabeth, I was left standing awkwardly in front alone. My bottom lip began to quiver. My teacher stepped toward me and leaned down, towering over me to ask my name. I was the little girl who wanted to run out the door home to my momma. It's horrible to feel like you don't belong.

Sheth likely felt this way often when he was living in Lo-debar—wanting to run but not being able to leave. Over the years, I've grown to appreciate my name. Elizabeth means "my God is an oath" (Luke 1:5 NRSV).[1] Just as God was faithful in his oath to Elizabeth, who gave birth to John the Baptist in her old age, my life is also a testament to God's oath—His covenant of love.

Maybe your first name was the one your parents gave you, but probably soon thereafter you started accruing nicknames. My dad called me "Lisa Lollipop" because he said I was sweet. We called my daughter "Bean" because she loved green beans straight out of the can when she was five. We affectionately called my son "Stinky." He answered to this nickname proudly—though I'll leave the reason to your imagination.

You and I have lots of names and wear many hats. We're daughters and friends. Perhaps we're wives, mothers, sisters, or aunts. We work as bakers, notetakers, and rulemakers.

Of all your names and titles, which is most important to you?

Some people define themselves by their accomplishments. They have more awards than the Oscars ever presented for big-screen talent. Perhaps they look to knowledge to distinguish themselves, amassing more degrees than a thermometer. Knowledge may impress others here on earth, but it will pass away like a holiday (1 Corinthians 13:8). I've personally found knowledge to be more like underclothing. You may have it, but you don't need to show it.

While all our roles, talents, and knowledge may be helpful—even honorable—what is most important to our identity at every age and stage is being a child of God.

And because we are his children, God has sent the Spirit of his Son into our hearts, prompting us to call out, "Abba, Father."

—Galatians 4:6

Read Galatians 4:6 in the margin. What feelings does this verse evoke? What name are you most comfortable calling God?

If your earthly father fell short and was unloving, unkind, or unavailable, it's likely hard to think of God as your heavenly Father. *Abba* is a Hebrew term of endearment, much like "daddy" in English. Sheth answered to several names. He was daddy to Mica, son to Jonathan, and grandson to Saul. But Sheth's most important identifier was that he was beloved of the king.

Mephibosheth ate at the king's table as though he were one of David's own sons.

Read Isaiah 43:1 in the margin. Imagine your heavenly Father smiling and saying this to you. How does it make you feel?

"Do not fear, for I have redeemed you;
I have summoned you by name; you are mine."
—Isaiah 43:1 NIV

These words remind me of King David's words to Sheth. Immediately after greeting him by name, King David said, "Do not fear" (2 Samuel 9:7 ESV). Isaiah's words tell us that God calls each of us by name. I'm wonderfully amazed by this because I struggle to remember names. This verse also makes me wonder which of my names God will use—my formal name, nickname, or something altogether different.

When we meet someone new, one of the first greetings they offer is their name. Names matter. They open the door to relationship. In Exodus 33:11, we're told that "the Lord would speak to Moses face to face, as one speaks to a friend." And in John 15:15, Jesus tells us that we, too, are called His friends. The intimacy Moses experienced was not just for him but is offered to us as well.

For weeks now, we've been meeting with God five days a week, and He has been revealing His heart to us. There was a pivotal moment in Moses's journey when God revealed something even more personal: His name.

But Moses protested, "If I go to the people of Israel and tell them, 'The God of your ancestors has sent me to you,' they will ask me, 'What is his name?' Then what should I tell them?"

God replied to Moses, "I AM WHO I AM. Say this to the people of Israel: I AM has sent me to you."

—Exodus 3:13-14

Read Exodus 3:13-14. What thoughts and emotions surface when you read God's response to Moses?

When I first pondered this years ago, "*I AM WHO I AM*" seemed hard to wrap my mind around. It's large and lofty. When someone asks me who I am, I have a feet-on-the-ground answer. *I am* David's wife. *I am* the mother of Alyssa and Garrett and mother-in-love to Robert and Bailey. *I am* Elijah and Gideon's GiGi.

Thankfully, God goes on to ground His identity for us in the same way, giving us something we can hold on to.

Look up Exodus 3:15 and fill in the blanks:

God also said to Moses, "Say this to the people of Israel: Yahweh,the God of your ancestors—the God of ____________________, *the God of* ______________, *and the God of* ______________— *has sent me to you.*

This is my eternal name,
my name to remember for all generations."

God cherishes being our Yahweh—the God who draws near; the One whose very name, YHWH, whispers breath and presence. YHWH is the One who sees you, stays with you, and loves you without wavering. These four sacred letters form what is called the tetragrammaton, a name so holy that ancient Israel spoke it with awe. It means "I AM," the God who simply *is* with you—steady, faithful, unchanging.

We are children of the great "I AM." Being a child of God is my foundation and my most life-identifying title! It's strong and unchanging—unlike my other names that change over time—because God is strong and unchanging. You are His child too. And when you are a child of the great *I* AM, you can say with confidence, "*I am* a child of the King."

What verb tense is "I am"? What does this say to you about God?

As a lover of words, the use of the present tense is significant to me. In Revelation 1:8, we read, "*I am* the Alpha and the Omega—the beginning and the end" (emphasis added). God didn't say, "I *was* the alpha and I *will be* the omega," because He is *present* in both our past and our future. Wherever our lives take us, we need not fear because our King is already there.

I can rest because the great I am is beside me wherever I am! And He's beside you too.

Worldly titles can change quicker than the winds that bring tornadoes to my home in Kansas City. What is unchanging is how the King of kings feels about you and me.

"Can a mother forget her nursing child? Can she feel no love for the child she has borne? But even if that were possible, I would not forget you! See, I have written your name on the palms of my hands."

—Isaiah 49:15-16a

Read Isaiah 49:15-16a in the margin. Take a moment to envision your name written on God's palms. Is it "tattooed"? Is it written in scrolling cursive letters? Describe it below.

While this is anthropomorphic language (human terms used to describe God), it carries deep comfort to help us feel the certainty of God's covenant love. Even if the most devoted mother could forget, God cannot. Your name is not written in ink and is more permanent than a tattoo, for it is "engraved" in God's eternal being—an unerasable assurance of His faithful, personal remembrance.

Just as King David called Mephibosheth by name, our King will call us by a new name when He greets us someday at His table (Revelation 2:17)! Our "new name" is Christ's deeply personal gift, whispered only to the heart He has redeemed. It reflects a healed identity, lovingly restored and fully known. This hidden name marks intimate belonging, cherished purpose, and the quiet joy of being completely seen and eternally held by God.

Enter into a time of worship. Scan this QR code to listen to "Who You Say I Am" by Hillsong Worship.

Reread this week's memory verse and fill in the blank as you allow this promise to fill your heart.

"I will_______________ all your children,
and they will enjoy great peace."
—Isaiah 54:13

Write your name in the blank and let this become the blessing Jesus whispers over your heart.

My beloved__________________, rest in My presence and listen as I whisper truth over you. Though the world gives you many names, none defines you like the one I have spoken since before time began: Mine. I see your brokenness, yet I call you dearly loved. Titles on earth will rise and fall, but your truest name is held safely in My hand, close to My heart. One day, I will speak that special name aloud, and you will know fully who you are in Me—My cherished, chosen child.

Now offer your response: *Jesus, . . .*

Day 3: Your New Calling

Biblical Foundations:
Micah 6:8; Matthew 28:16-20; Luke 6:38; Ephesians 2:10; 1 Timothy 2:3-4

Focus Scripture:
I urge you, first of all, to pray for all people. Ask God to help them; intercede on their behalf, and give thanks for them. Pray this way for kings and all who are in authority so that we can live peaceful and quiet lives marked by godliness and dignity. This is good and pleases God our Savior, who wants everyone to be saved and to understand the truth. —1 Timothy 2:1-4

While many have heard of King David, far fewer have heard of Mephibosheth. I believe God preserved Sheth's story so that we know even in our brokenness, we are beloved. Sheth was crippled as a child and lived hidden in fear until David sought him out, restored his dignity, and seated him at the king's table. His life whispers a truth meant for every one of us: Even in our most wounded places, we are cherished, chosen, and invited to sit with the King of kings.

In that same love, you and I are called to extend the invitation to the King's table to whomever would believe (John 3:16). Countless people feel too lost, lonely, or fearful to ever step into a church, yet they desperately need to hear that a seat at the King's table has been set for them too. As one who sits at the King's table, you have been given magnificent "invitations" to deliver to *whomever* you meet, *wherever* you go, and *whatever* their circumstances.

Look up 1 Timothy 2:1-4. Who does God long to see saved? (v. 4)

Take a moment to consider the people God has placed closest to your heart. Is there someone who hasn't yet experienced the joy of salvation? Write their name and the invitation of God's heart for them on the stationery below.

Paul's words to Timothy point us to the Great Commission, where Jesus reveals God's heart: a calling that extends to every nation, every people, every person.

"Therefore, go and make disciples of all the nations, baptizing them in the name of the Father and the Son and the Holy Spirit. Teach these new disciples to obey all the commands I have given you. And be sure of this: I am with you always, even to the end of the age."

—Matthew 28:19-20

Read Matthew 28:19-20. Do you feel called to invite others into discipleship? If so, explain how you are most comfortable extending this invitation. If not, what concerns are holding you back?

Calling this passage The Great Commission sounds far too formal to me. I'd rather think of it as Jesus's joyful invitation to help Him distribute invitations for others to belong to our family. After all, we all love to be invited! Jesus isn't asking us to be experts; He's asking us to be willing. When I hear the phrase "Go and make disciples of all the nations," my mind jumps to mission trips in far-off continents. But instead of beginning there, why not start somewhere beautifully ordinary?

Consider how many trips you make each week to the grocery store, the pharmacy, the gas station, or the big-box stores. Jot down an approximate number below.

What if all your ordinary outings became a series of mini mission trips—lots of little opportunities to scatter love, joy, peace, patience, kindness, gentleness, faithfulness, and self-control wherever you go? Imagine choosing to steady your responses to snippy cashiers or unhelpful associates even when frustrations rise, turning each moment into a quiet act of grace.

If you work outside the home, think of how many people you meet. What if you made it your quiet goal to offer each one a simple, sincere compliment? "You're so helpful." "You wear that outfit well." "I appreciate your outlook." Whatever feels natural to you. In all my years, I've never met a person who was offended by a genuine compliment.

When you train your eyes to look for someone to lift up, it becomes second nature. Before long, every outing becomes a chance to quietly brighten your corner of the world. You'll find your life changed by this new calling!

Read Ephesians 2:10 in the margin. What does this verse tell you about your calling?

For we are God's masterpiece. He has created us anew in Christ Jesus, ***so we can do the good things he planned for us long ago.***

—Ephesians 2:10 (emphasis added)

This verse reminds me that we each have purpose. We were born to do good! We're God's workmanship—His intentional, handcrafted creations—and that truth steadies our calling as women in every season of life. It means your calling isn't something you have to chase, prove, or perfect; it's something God has already prepared for you to walk in. Sometimes we make our calling far more complicated than it needs to be. But God keeps things beautifully simple.

Look up Micah 6:8. Here our calling is distilled into just three things. Write them below.

1. ____

2. ____

3. ____

Let your heart receive this beautiful truth: We are invited—right now and for all eternity—to sit at the King's table. The invitation is not only for a distant heavenly future but also for every present moment in our everyday lives, just as Mephibosheth was invited to sit regularly at King David's table.

Jesus announced that God's kingdom had already begun breaking into the world through His ministry, declaring, "The time promised by God has come at last! . . . The Kingdom of God is near! Repent of your sins and believe the Good News!" (Mark 1:15). His words remind us that God's reign is not a far-off dream but a present reality we're welcomed into with open arms.

Jesus described the kingdom of God not as a physical place on a map but as the active, loving rule of God wherever hearts yield to Him (Matthew 6:10; 12:28). He said the kingdom is "among you" and also "in your midst" (Luke 17:20-21 NIV). This is a work God does inside us and among us, shaping the way we live in community.

This kingdom is both already and not yet: already present as we practice justice, mercy, and love, yet not fully realized until the day when God's will is perfectly fulfilled (Hebrews 2:8-9; 1 Corinthians 13:12). Every act of obedience, every moment of compassion, every quiet surrender becomes a small but powerful sign of God's reign taking root. And so, as women of faith who follow our King, we live in this beautiful tension—experiencing glimpses of the Kingdom now while longing for the fullness still to come.

The prophet Isaiah wrote of a future banquet, a great celebration where all things will be made right.

Read Isaiah 25:6-9 and describe this banquet in your own words—and the emotions it stirs in your heart.

Until that day, we taste the kingdom each time we gather, pray, serve, and love (Acts 2:42-47). The King's table is set before us even now, inviting us to live as daughters of the King and to invite others in our communities and our world to join us. One of the best ways to do that is simply to share our own stories of hope.

Read 1 Peter 3:15b in the margin. When you consider your hope as a believer, what story of how Jesus met you in your deepest need comes to mind? Briefly describe it below.

If someone asks about your hope as a believer, always be ready to explain it.

—1 Peter 3:15b

Peter was a practical man. His words urge us to be ready to share our story of how Jesus met us when we needed Him most. I shared mine in week 3, describing the time when I felt "less than enough" as a pharmacist, wife, and mother until, one day, Jesus met me tenderly through the miracle of the feeding of the five thousand. At my lowest point, He asked for my two goldfish crackers and five crumbly croutons. When I felt uncounted and unworthy, He saw me and taught me that *with Him* I am more than enough.

I wish I could hear *your* story of hope! Peter reminds us that our stories matter—not because they're polished, but because they reveal how Jesus meets us in real life. Maybe He met you in fear. Maybe He carried you through loss. Maybe He surprised you with joy. Maybe He's still writing your chapter of hope. Whatever your story looks like, it's enough. It's powerful. And it will encourage someone else. What you may see as ordinary can become healing in God's hands. Rest in knowing that Jesus is with you. Ask Him to give you the courage to share with others the joy that comes from belonging to His eternal family.

Enter into a time of worship. Scan this QR code to listen to "House of the Lord" by Phil Wickham.

Reread this week's memory verse and fill in the blanks as you allow this promise to fill your heart.

"I will __________ all your ______________,
and they will enjoy great peace."
—Isaiah 54:13

Write your name in the blank and let this become the blessing Jesus whispers over your heart.

My beloved ______________, I have invited you into My Kingdom—here and now, and forever in heaven. You are Mine, and I have chosen you to carry My invitation to others. Do not underestimate your worth in My work. Every person you meet is someone I long to welcome. This is your purpose: to shine My presence, extend My invitation, and draw hearts toward Me. Walk in confidence, knowing I have commissioned you and equipped you with My love.

Now offer your response: *Jesus, . . .*

Day 4: Your New Legacy

Biblical Foundations:
Jeremiah 17:8; Acts 9:38-42; 1 Corinthians 12:4-6; 1 Peter 4:10

Focus Scripture:
There are different kinds of spiritual gifts, but the same Spirit is the source of them all. There are different kinds of service, but we serve the same Lord. God works in different ways, but it is the same God who does the work in all of us.
—1 Corinthians 12:4-6

Yesterday we learned that our calling is less about traveling far and more about opening our hearts right where we are. Passing out invitations to the King's table simply means noticing those around us who feel unseen, overwhelmed, or unworthy, and gently sharing that Jesus has saved them a seat.

We "go" when we walk across the room, send a text, offer a prayer, or share a story of God's faithfulness. We "make disciples" when we listen well, love consistently, and point others to the One who transforms lives. And we "baptize" by helping women step into a new identity—beloved, chosen, welcomed. This calling isn't heavy. It's holy hospitality—one invitation at a time.

Today we turn to our legacy—the fragrance of our lives that lingers long after our footsteps fade. Your legacy is the sweet aroma of Christ carried forward through the people you've touched and the faith you've lived. It's like an orchard planted beside a river with intention: rows of trees nurtured over time, offering fruit you may never personally taste.

Read Jeremiah 17:8 in the margin for a description of those who trust in the Lord. Sketch the scene below.

"They are like trees planted along a riverbank, with roots that reach deep into the water. Such trees are not bothered by the heat or worried by long months of drought. Their leaves stay green, and they never stop producing fruit."
—Jeremiah 17:8

The next generation walks among those branches, gathering what your life produced—wisdom, courage, compassion, and faith that continues to bear much fruit. I imagine Mephibosheth never dreamed that women like us—in the twenty-first century—would be gathering around his story, studying his life to learn what it means to leave a legacy of love. His world was full of shadows and sharp edges, yet here we are, finding hope in the very places he felt most broken.

Sheth inherited quite a mixed legacy. On one side stood his grandfather, a tormented king who tried to kill David numerous times. On the other stood his father, a man known for fierce loyalty and unwavering friendship to David. Jonathan had several brothers, yet David loved him with a closeness deeper than brotherhood. What a contrast of histories Sheth carried in one fragile life, yet our loving King preserved his radiant legacy, which offers us a living picture of how He invites us to His table—not when we're polished or strong, but in the middle of our brokenness.

Mephibosheth's legacy reminds me of another—carried by a woman who was not well known, not from a royal line, and without a famous husband or family name to secure her place in history. That makes her wonderfully relatable to women like us: ordinary daughters invited into an extraordinary story, quietly faithful yet seen by the King.

She needed friends. She longed for her life to matter. Her dreams and desires echo the ones tucked into our hearts as we hope to leave legacies of love. She became known for something ordinary in her day: she sewed. Yet she stands apart from every other woman in the Bible. She is the only named woman raised from death to life (though Jairus's unnamed twelve-year-old daughter was also raised), and the only woman explicitly called a *mathetria*—the feminine form of the Hebrew word for "disciple" (Acts 9:36).[2]

Her common name was Dorcas, and her common life became uncommon in God's hands. She left a legacy that will be remembered for eternity.

Read the story of Dorcas in Acts 9:36-42. What did the widows do when she died?

Dorcas—as well as her Hebrew name Tabitha—means "gazelle," and she truly lived up to it. Dorcas was graceful, quick to help, always moving toward anyone in need. She was known for overflowing kindness and acts of mercy that wrapped vulnerable women in warm dignity. When she died, her friends—the widows she had clothed and comforted—stood around her weeping, holding up the garments she had lovingly sewn. They sent for Peter with desperate hope that God might move through him. Although Peter had healed people of ailments, Dorcas was the first person he resurrected from death. And her resurrection had a ripple effect in the early church.

What was the legacy of Dorcas's life?

Dorcas's life—and resurrection—became a legacy of God's powerful compassion and the quiet power of a faithful servant. Both Dorcas and Sheth left legacies that can inspire us! Across the sixty-six books of Scripture, just a handful are devoted to Sheth, yet our King preserved his legacy, offering us a vivid picture of how He loves us.

Similarly, Dorcas's story is told in just a few verses, yet her legacy changed the face of the early church. *Many* came to believe after the miracle of her resurrection, all because poor widows who had been touched by her love asked for a miracle. Her resurrection precedes a greater miracle—the soon-to-come moment on a rooftop in Joppa when Peter will receive a vision that opens the door for the early church to welcome Gentiles into what had been an exclusively Jewish faith.

Dorcas sowed seeds of kindness. We are each called to sow, though we may not sew with a needle. Sometimes finding our God-given gifts can feel like searching for a needle in a haystack. But here's the truth: God has entrusted each of us with more gifts and talents than we'll ever fully use in one lifetime. Still, we can be hesitant to name them. As a young person, I never would have called myself a writer or a teacher because I didn't have a degree in English or education. Yet even without those particular degrees, I use both gifts regularly. God ordains gifts long before we recognize them.

There are different kinds of spiritual gifts, but the same Spirit is the source of them all. There are different kinds of service, but we serve the same Lord. God works in different ways, but it is the same God who does the work in all of us.

—1 Corinthians 12:4-6

Read 1 Corinthians 12:4-6. Of what do these verses assure us?

What gifts can you name that God has stitched into your story? (If you're not sure, keep reading!)

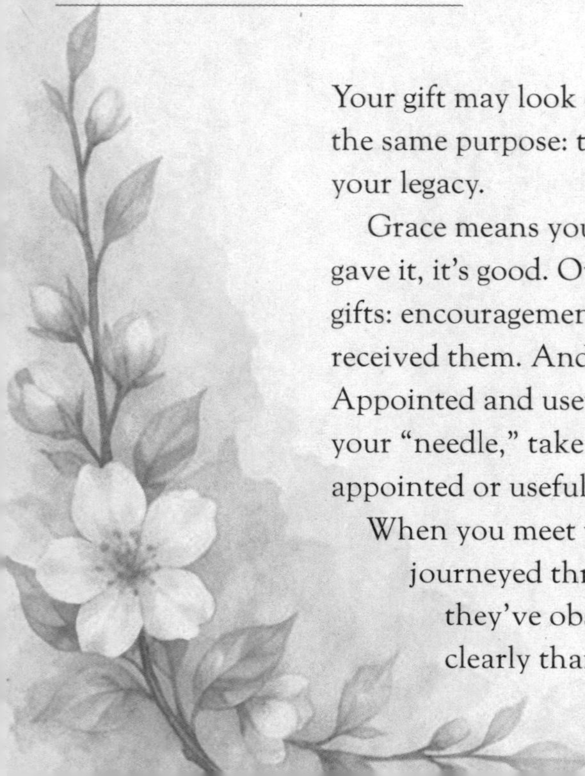

Your gift may look different, but it comes from the same Spirit and serves the same purpose: to build up the body of Christ for eternity. This can be your legacy.

Grace means your gift doesn't need a diploma to be valid. If God gave it, it's good. Over the years, I've come to recognize some additional gifts: encouragement, hospitality, and gift-giving. I didn't earn them; I received them. And when I use them, I feel profound joy! Alive. Aligned. Appointed and useful to the Kingdom. So if you're still searching for your "needle," take inventory. When do you feel most alive, aligned, and appointed or useful for God's plans and purposes?

When you meet with your group this week, ask those who have journeyed through this study with you what gifts and talents they've observed in you. Oftentimes, others see our gifts more clearly than we do—and they're more likely to name them.

Read 1 Peter 4:10 in the margin. Why have we been given spiritual gifts? How does this make you feel?

God has given each of you a gift from his great variety of spiritual gifts. Use them well to serve one another.

—1 Peter 4:10

Your gift isn't just for you; it's your legacy for the church, for the hurting, for the world. When you find your gift, your needle, use it. Use it to uplift the church, to help or encourage others, to speak life. You don't have to be credentialed to leave a world-changing legacy. You don't have to be perfect to be purposeful. When you name your gift and use it well to serve others, that's where joy lives. That's where your legacy begins!

Reread this week's memory verse and fill in the blanks as you allow this promise to fill your heart.

"I will ____________ all your ________________,

and they will ______________ great peace."

—Isaiah 54:13

Write your name in the blank and let this become the blessing Jesus whispers over your heart.

My beloved ________________________, I am with you in this moment, but My calling for you stretches far beyond today. I have placed beautiful gifts within you. Discover them with joy. Name them without fear. Share them freely. As you offer these gifts, you shine My light into places only you can reach. What you carry is not small; it is part of the legacy I am shaping through you. Claim every gift for My glory, and together we will touch hearts and impact eternity.

Now offer your response: *Jesus, . . .*

Enter into a time of worship. Scan this QR code to listen to "Made for More" by Josh Baldwin.

Day 5: Rest in God's Love

Biblical Foundations:

2 Samuel 4:4; 9:6-13; 16:1-4; 19:24-30; 1 Chronicles 8:34; 9:40; Zephaniah 3:17; 1 Corinthians 13:11-13; Ephesians 3:18-20; Colossians 3:2

Focus Scripture:

When I was a child, I spoke and thought and reasoned as a child. But when I grew up, I put away childish things.Now we see things imperfectly, like puzzling reflections in a mirror, but then we will see everything with perfect clarity.All that I know now is partial and incomplete, but then I will know everything completely, just as God now knows me completely. Three things will last forever—faith, hope, and love—and the greatest of these is love.

—1 Corinthians 13:11-13

One of my favorite TV channels is Home & Garden TV (HGTV). I enjoy the renovation shows, but what I like most is *the reveal*—those last ten minutes when the before-and-after shots flash across the screen and you can finally see what all the waiting, dust, and disruption were for.

Maybe that's why I've been anticipating this day for six weeks. It feels like a "spiritual reveal"—a tender moment when we pause, look back, and realize that God has been quietly restoring Sheth's story and our story all along. He took the *bad* and, with His gentle hands, worked it into *good*. His story makes me pause and wonder: Where am I holding wounds of my past—regrets, failures, and fear-shaped memories that feel heavy—and how might these be the very places in me that God longs to transform into good?

How about you? What is one wound or heavy memory you carry, and how might God be inviting you to see it as a place where He wants to bring healing and new life?

Real life isn't a one-hour HGTV renovation. Spiritual renovations take time. They're messy. They stretch across seasons—sometimes decades. This is the process of sanctification. But God is faithful in the slow work.

Mephibosheth's story is proof. It's messy, but the ending is tender and deeply heartwarming. At the center of it all is a life-changing truth: Even in the places where we feel fractured, overlooked, or not-enough, we're cherished, chosen, and invited to sit with the King of kings. King David lifted Sheth up when he was a young man in need of kindness. Years later, Sheth lifted David up when he was an old man in need of encouragement. Their lives became a circle of grace and an example for us.

Think of someone who once blessed you. How might you be a blessing to them now? Write their name and your thoughts below.

God invites us to embody *hesed*—loyal, compassionate love—to others who, like Sheth, need to be lifted up. Loving others the way God loves us is one of the ways God overcomes evil with good in our world. When we love others, God brings Romans 8:28 to life through our hands and hearts. And no matter what brokenness we've walked through on this earth, we can rest in the promise that good wins in the end (Revelation 22)!

Here's the beautiful truth: Our brokenness doesn't make us any less loved; if anything, it makes us even more cherished. Brokenness is hard, yet brokenness that brings us to our knees is holy. There's no better place for us to be than kneeling before our King. When Mephibosheth bowed, his life changed for the better. Our lives begin to change, too, when we finally realize just how deeply we are loved. Scripture is really one big love story: God so loved the world, and that includes *you*.

I want to leave you with three of my favorite verses that paint a rich picture of the beautiful way God loves us.

Match the reference on the left with the corresponding verse(s) on the right. Then draw a heart beside your favorite.

Zephaniah 3:17	Love never fails. But where there are prophecies, they will cease; where there are tongues, they will be stilled; where there is knowledge, it will pass away.
Ephesians 3:18-20	And may you have the power to understand, as all God's people should, how wide, how long, how high, and how deep his love is. May you experience the love of Christ, though it is too great to understand fully. Then you will be made complete with all the fullness of life and power that comes from God. Now all glory to God, who is able, through his mighty power at work within us, to accomplish infinitely more than we might ask or think.
1 Corinthians 13:8 (NIV)	"For the LORD your God is living among you. He is a mighty savior. He will take delight in you with gladness. With his love, he will calm all your fears. He will rejoice over you with joyful songs."

You may have many spiritual gifts. You may have great knowledge having completed many Bible studies like this one. You may be gifted to teach. But all these gifts will fade while love remains.

Whether you've only skimmed the pages of this study or you've completed every exercise, God looks at you with love. Regardless of your story, God wants you to experience the fullness of His love for you. He will keep inviting you to His table every single day because He wants you to know that your brokenness doesn't matter to Him.

We come with stories that haven't been fully mended, and still He calls us by name with compassion. Not one of us is turned away. Not one of us is overlooked. At the King's table, the dropped are lifted, the wounded are welcomed, and the imperfect are embraced.

So as we end this study, we can carry this truth in our hearts: We do not sit at His table because we are whole; we sit there because Jesus is. Our King has made room for us. He delights in us and will never stop inviting us closer.

When our days are filled with broken dreams, broken health, and broken hearts, He gently redirects our gaze. On earth, brokenness will always be part of the story in some measure. But in heaven, brokenness will be *restored*!

With Sheth's story in mind, read 1 Corinthians 13:11-13. How do you see his story reflected in these verses?

How have you experienced God's love, faithfulness, or restoration in your own life during this study? What have you heard God whisper to you these past six weeks that you don't want to forget?

Never forget you always have a seat *at the King's table: where the broken are beloved!*

Reread this week's memory verse and fill in the blanks as you allow this promise to fill your heart.

"I will ____________ *all your* ________________,

and they will ____________ *great*

____________."

—Isaiah 54:13

Enter into a time of worship. Scan this QR code to listen to "Perfectly Loved" by Rachael Lampa.

Write your name in the blank and let this become the blessing Jesus whispers over your heart.

*My beloved*________________*, nothing you bring Me is too broken for My hands. I gather every shard and hold you as My beloved, now and always. As we walk forward together, trust that I am weaving even the painful pieces into good. One day, in the home I'm preparing for you, every wound will be healed, every tear redeemed, and everything will be made whole in My presence. And until then, I invite you to eat at my table continually, enjoying the fullness of my love.*

Now offer your response: *Jesus, . . .*

Week 6

Video Viewer Guide

1. The Love Challenge: Make every ordinary outing a series of ________ ______________ ________ —small, intentional moments to scatter love, joy, peace, patience, kindness, goodness, gentleness, faithfulness, and self-control wherever you go.

2. Barnabas shows us that ________________ doesn't have to be ________________.

3. Barnabas wasn't driven by status; he was driven by the Spirit, knowing that God can ______________ and ______________ anyone.

4. Barnabas saw ______________ where others saw ____________.

5. You don't need to be a preacher, a scholar, or a leader to be an ________________ like Barnabas.

6. Naming your gifts and talents isn't ________________; it's acknowledging the __________________, the Gift Giver.

Video Viewer Guide Answers

Week 1

1. Me | me
2. part of life | peace
3. mature
4. because | produce
5. is good | for the good
6. beloved

Week 2

1. action
2. liberating
3. sin
4. forgiveness
5. big | small
6. depletion
7. Fear | fatigue

Week 3

1. fear
2. have | insufficient
3. leftovers
4. broken | beloved
5. enough | more than enough

Week 4

1. passive | powerful
2. love | action
3. rescuing her heart
4. resting | rushing
5. peace
6. comparison | worship
7. do | rest

Week 5

1. fickle | family
2. gratitude | resentment
3. comfort | God
4. defends | misunderstand
5. truth
6. gain | give

Week 6

1. mini mission trips
2. failure | final
3. redeem |reshape
4. potential | risk
5. encourager
6. arrogant | Artist

Leader Guide

This leader guide is provided to help you facilitate a six-week study of *At the King's Table: Where the Broken Are Beloved.* For each week, there are five lessons that combine the study of Scripture with personal reflection and application. On average, each lesson can be completed in about twenty to thirty minutes. Completing these lessons each week will prepare the women for the video they will watch and the discussion they will have together during the group session. (See page 4 for instructions on how to access the streaming video sessions.)

Be sure that the women have their books and complete the lessons for Week 1 prior to your first session. Or, if desired, you can add an extra week for an introductory session, where you can distribute books, get to know one another, and introduce your group to the study. That would extend the study to a total of seven weeks.

Group Session Format

You are encouraged to use this leader material however it best serves you and your group—whether that is following it exactly as written or adapting it for your group. Each group session outline is formatted for either a 60-minute or 90-minute group session.

60-Minute Format

Welcome and Opening Prayer	5 minutes
Icebreaker	5 minutes
Video	20 minutes
Group Discussion	25 minutes
Closing Prayer	5 minutes

90-Minute Format

Welcome and Opening Prayer	5–10 minutes
Icebreaker	5 minutes
Video	20 minutes
Group Discussion	35 minutes
Deeper Conversation	15 minutes
Closing Prayer	5 minutes

As you can see, the 90-minute format is identical to the 60-minute format but allows more time for the welcome/opening prayer and group discussion plus a Deeper Conversation exercise for small groups. Again, feel free to adapt or modify either of these formats, as well as the individual elements themselves, in any way to meet the specific needs and preferences of your group.

Here is a brief overview of the elements included in both formats:

Welcome and Opening Prayer

(5–10 minutes, depending on session length)

Create a warm, welcoming environment as the women gather before the session begins. Consider either lighting a candle, providing coffee or other refreshments, or playing worship music, or all of these. (Bring a smartphone or tablet and a portable speaker if desired.) Be sure to provide nametags if the women do not know one another or if you have new participants in your group. Then, when you are ready to begin, open the group in prayer before you begin your time.

Icebreaker

(5 minutes)

Use the icebreaker to briefly engage the women in the topic while helping them feel comfortable with one another.

Video

(20 minutes)

Next, watch the week's video segment together. Be sure to direct participants to the Video Viewer Guide in this book, which they may complete as they watch the video. (Answers are provided on page 214.)

Group Discussion

(25–35 minutes, depending on session length)

After watching the video, choose from the questions provided to facilitate group discussion (questions are provided for both the video segment and the weekly lessons).

Note that more material is provided than you will have time to include. Before the session, select which questions you want to ask, putting a check mark beside them. Reflect on each question and make some notes in the margins to share during your discussion time. Page references are provided for those questions that relate to specific questions in the weekly lessons. For these questions, invite group members to turn to the pages indicated. Participants will need Bibles in order to look up various Scriptures.

Depending on the number of women in your group and the level of their participation, you may not have time to cover everything you have selected, and that is okay. Rather than attempting to bulldoze through, follow the Spirit's lead and be open to where the Spirit takes the conversation. Remember that your role is not to have all the answers but to encourage discussion and sharing.

Deeper Conversation

(15 minutes)

If your group is meeting for 90 minutes, use this exercise for deeper sharing in small groups—dividing into groups of two or three if your group is smaller, or discussing around tables if your group is larger. This is a time for women to share more intimately and build connections with one another. Give a two-minute warning before time is up so that the groups may wrap up their discussion.

Closing Prayer

(5 minutes)

Close by leading the group in prayer. If you'd like, invite the women to briefly name prayer requests. As the study progresses, you might encourage members to participate in the Closing Prayer by praying out loud for one another and the requests given. Ask the women to volunteer to pray for specific requests, or have each woman pray for the woman on her right or left. Make sure nametags are visible so that group members do not feel awkward if they do not remember someone's name.

If your group is larger, you might prefer to have each woman write her prayer request and her name on an index card and exchange cards with another person in the group.

Enhancing Your Study

A bonus feature of the study is a weekly recipe chosen to echo the week's theme, so that when you gather in sweet fellowship you can "taste and see that the LORD is good" (Psalm 34:8a). Consider it an invitation to not only know about God's goodness but also experience it personally. My hope is that with your invitation, someone in the group will volunteer to prepare the recipe each week and bring it to your group meeting to share. You can ask for a volunteer weekly or create a sign-up sheet that the women can fill in during your first session—perhaps bringing the first dish yourself.

Because we are called to serve, I also encourage you to invite everyone to bring an item each week for a food pantry so that others can know in a tangible way that God loves them and desires to provide for *their* table. Check with your church or local food pantry for suggested items.

Finally, I would be delighted to meet with your group for a fifteen-minute video chat during your last session. With advance notice, I may be able to arrange this if schedules permit. Feel free to reach out through the Connect tab at lisawilt.com.

Leader Helps

Preparing for the Sessions

- Choose either the 60- or 90-minute format.
- Communicate dates and times to your group members in advance of the first session.
- Ensure group members receive their workbooks and complete the first week's lessons prior to your first session (if not having an introductory session). Send a welcome and reminder if possible.
- Prepare your meeting space (or set up a virtual meeting and share the link).
- Pray for your group and each group member by name. Ask God to work in the life of every woman in your group.
- Complete the weekly lessons yourself, review the session outline, and make notes in the margins to share in your discussion time.

Leading the Sessions

- Personally welcome and greet each woman as she arrives (whether in person or online). You might want to have a sign-up list for the women to record their names and contact information.
- At the start of each session, ask the women to turn off or silence their cell phones (or eliminate other distractions if meeting online).
- Always start on time. Honor the time of those who are punctual.
- Encourage everyone to complete the weekly lessons and participate fully, but don't put anyone on the spot. Be prepared to offer a personal example or answer if no one else responds at first.
- Facilitate but don't dominate. Remember that if you talk most of the time, group members may tend to listen rather than to engage. Your task is to encourage conversation and keep the discussion moving.
- If someone monopolizes the conversation, kindly thank her for sharing and ask if anyone else has any insights.
- Try not to interrupt, judge, or minimize anyone's comments or input.
- Remember that you are not expected to be the expert or have all the answers. Acknowledge that all of you are on this journey together, with the Holy Spirit as your leader and guide. If issues or questions arise that you don't feel equipped to handle or answer, talk with the pastor or a staff member at your church.
- Don't rush to fill the silence. If no one speaks right away, it's okay to wait for someone to answer. After a moment, ask, "Would anyone be willing to share?" If no one responds, try asking the question again a different way—or offer a brief response and ask if anyone has anything to add.
- Encourage good discussion, but don't be timid about calling time on a particular question and moving ahead. Part of your responsibility is to keep the group on track. If you decide to spend extra time on a

given question, consider skipping or spending less time on another question in order to stay on schedule.

- End on time. If you are running over, give members the opportunity to leave if they need to. Then wrap up as quickly as you can.
- Thank the women for coming and let them know you're looking forward to seeing them next time.
- Be prepared for some women to want to hang out and talk at the end. If you need everyone to leave by a certain time, communicate this at the beginning of the group session. If you are meeting in a church during regularly scheduled activities, be aware of nursery closing times.

Session Outlines

WEEK 1

Memory Verse

But he was hurt because of us; he suffered so.
Our wrongdoing wounded and *crushed him.*
He endured the breaking that made us whole.
The injuries he suffered became our healing.
—Isaiah 53:5 *The Voice (emphasis added)*

The Big Picture

This week we explore some ways that we, like Mephibosheth, experience brokenness and how they can remind us of our need for healing from One greater than ourselves. Here are some key takeaways:

- **Day 1:** When we view Mephibosheth's physical brokenness through the lens of covenant friendship and God's steadfast *hesed* love, we're reminded that our own broken bodies and stories are held and redeemed by God's unwavering love and faithfulness.
- **Day 2:** The story of Jesus's encounter with the woman at the well offers tender insight into how God sees our brokenness—and how He can redeem it, using our wounds to build bridges that reach others with the good news of His unfailing love.
- **Day 3:** Just as Mephibosheth's broken body contributed to broken thinking, our own wounds and fears can distort our minds; but with the help of the Holy Spirit and the Holy Scriptures, God can renew our thinking, quiet the lies, and lead us into true freedom.
- **Day 4:** Just as Sheth's debilitating injury resulted from fear and led to his seclusion, our broken world can cripple us with fear; yet God lovingly invites us to humble ourselves, pray, and turn to Him so He can heal and restore us (2 Chronicles 7:14).
- **Day 5:** Even in our brokenness—body, mind, or spirit—God meets us in our fear and weakness, giving us strength, hope, and the assurance that we are never alone.

Welcome and Opening Prayer *(5–10 minutes, depending on session length)*
Welcome each woman as she arrives (or joins online) and encourage the women to talk informally until you are ready to open the group in prayer. Use this prayer or offer one of your own:

> *Loving God, as we gather to begin our study, we acknowledge our brokenness—in body, mind, and spirit. Open our hearts today to Your unfailing love. Help us trust that even in our weakness, You are close, rescuing us and guiding us to healing and wholeness. In Jesus's name we pray. Amen.*

Icebreaker *(5 minutes)*
Invite the women to share short responses to the following question:

- In what small or everyday way have you experienced the brokenness of this world in your own life recently?

Video *(20 minutes)*
Play the week 1 video. Invite participants to complete the Video Viewer Guide on page 44 as they watch.

Group Discussion *(25–35 minutes, depending on session length)*
Video

- Review the following verses Lisa shared in the video: John 16:33; Isaiah 43:2; Romans 5:3-5; and James 1:24. What encouragement do these verses offer us for living in this broken world?
- Lisa read Romans 8:28 and said that "God lovingly gathers every thread and works them together for the good of those who trust Him." How have you seen this promise in your life?
- How does it make you feel to know that your scars don't disqualify you but make you precious in God's eyes?

Weekly Lessons
Day 1

- What were the three covenant promises between Jonathan and David? (pages 14–16) Why is their friendship important to the story of Mephibosheth?

- Have someone read aloud Isaiah 54:10. How does Lisa's explanation of the meaning of *hesed* deepen your appreciation of the promise of this verse?
- How does the brief parenthetical reference to Mephibosheth in 2 Samuel 4:4 shape your understanding of his identity and vulnerability in this unfolding story of David's rise to the throne?

Day 2

- What does Jesus's interaction with the woman at the well reveal about God's heart toward our brokenness?
- When has God used an unexpected person to speak a humble, heartfelt blessing of the good news into your life? And how has God used the brokenness in *your* story to reach people? (page 25)

Day 3

- What do our thought patterns have to do with the restoration and wholeness God desires for us? How do Romans 12:2 and Philippians 4:8 speak into this, providing helpful instruction?
- If you carried the truth of Philippians 4:8 with you, how might it change your thinking? (page 30)

Day 4

- What do we learn from 2 Samuel 4 about why the entire nation of Israel was paralyzed by fear—and how fear might have played a part in Mephibosheth's injury?
- Like Sheth's nurse and Jehosheba, how can you use your influence—however quiet or hidden—to preserve life, truth, and hope? (page 36)

Day 5

- What is one practical way you could apply the truth of 1 John 4:18 in your life? (page 38)
- Read aloud Romans 8:26 and Psalm 34:18. How do these promises offer you comfort today?

Deeper Conversation *(15 minutes)*

Divide into smaller groups for deeper conversation:

- This week we explored some of the ways we experience brokenness—broken bodies (physical ailments), broken relationships, broken thinking, the brokenness of the world, and a broken spirit. Of these five categories, which one resonates most strongly with you today, and why?

Closing Prayer *(5 minutes)*

Loving God, You see and understand our pain because you entered into the brokenness of this world Yourself. Thank You that we are never alone in our suffering, and that our hope rests in your unfailing love. You not only walk with us through the pain, but you renew our minds, quiet our fears, and give us courage and strength for each day. Draw near to us now and restore us again. In Jesus's name we pray. Amen.

WEEK 2

Memory Verse

"Do not be afraid or discouraged, for the LORD will personally go ahead of you. He will be with you; he will neither fail you nor abandon you."

—Deuteronomy 31:8

The Big Picture

This week we consider how we, like Mephibosheth, often feel we have fallen from favor and need to hide our hurts. And the good news for us is that Jesus was broken so we can be made whole. Here are some key takeaways:

- **Day 1:** Life's disappointments can leave us feeling forgotten or unworthy, yet God's covenant love reminds us that we are His beloved—invited to draw near, be healed, and find our worth in His voice alone.
- **Day 2:** Like Mephibosheth, we may carry shame or labels that are not ours. God sees our brokenness with compassion, invites us to receive His healing, and transforms even our deepest hurts into a place of redemption.
- **Day 3:** Like Mephibosheth and Hagar, even in our lowest, loneliest moments, God sees us, meets us with compassion, and calls us out of hiding with His gentle, unhurried grace.
- **Day 4:** Like Mephibosheth, even when we feel orphaned, overwhelmed, or burdened by undeserved pain, God holds us steady, lifts our hearts, and invites us to live "freely and lightly" in His care (Matthew 11:30 MSG).
- **Day 5:** Fear can keep us hidden like Mephibosheth, yet God's truth and presence give us the courage to step out, embrace our calling, and act boldly for His purposes.

Welcome and Opening Prayer *(5–10 minutes, depending on session length)*

Welcome each woman as she arrives (or joins online) and encourage the women to talk informally until you are ready to open the group in prayer. Use this prayer or offer one of your own:

Loving God, we're so grateful that You see us in every place of brokenness, shame, and fear—and you meet us with compassion and grace. As we gather today, open our hearts to Your healing, lift our spirits from hiding, and give us courage to step into the purpose You have prepared for us. May we rest in the assurance that we are Your beloved—held and never alone. Amen.

Icebreaker *(5 minutes)*

Invite the women to share short responses to the following prompt:

- Share a time when you experienced FOMO (fear of missing out) or imposter syndrome.

Video *(20 minutes)*

Play the week 2 video. Invite participants to complete the Video Viewer Guide on page 80 as they watch.

Group Discussion *(25–35 minutes, depending on session length)*

Video

- How does recognizing that struggles, mistakes, and hardships are part of being human—as we see in Mephibosheth's story—affect the way you view your own challenges or those of others?
- How do you relate to Elijah's story? How does it encourage you?
- What are some ways we can minister to others through nourishing care and presence? When have you offered, and received, this kind of care lately?

Weekly Lessons

Day 1

- Which of the examples of "falling from favor" that Lisa shared resonates most strongly with you, and why? (pages 50-51)
- What does David's question in 2 Samuel 9:1 reveal about his heart? (page 51)
- In Mark 5:25-34, Jesus calls the bleeding woman "daughter," a tender name full of care and affirmation. How does hearing God call you His beloved daughter in a personal, tender way change the way you see yourself, your worth, or your struggles?

Day 2

- What does the name *Mephibosheth* mean? How do both his name and his story remind us that despite what the world may think, whisper, or shout about our broken places, we are never too damaged for our King?
- In your own words, how would you explain the difference between shame and guilt? How does John 10:10 speak to our struggle with shame? How can we embrace our identity as God's beloved rather than being defined by our mistakes?

Day 3

- Read aloud 2 Samuel 9:4a and review the story of Hagar (Genesis 16:1-7). What connection do you see between these two Scriptures?
- What is your familiar Lo-debar, and when do you find yourself most tempted to hide there? (page 64)
- Even if it's hard to believe at times, how might it change your perspective to consider that in every Lo-debar moment, God sees you, understands your struggle, and moves toward you with compassion?

Day 4

- Read 2 Samuel 9:4b. What was the name of the man in whose home Mephibosheth was living, and what does his name mean? How do you imagine that Mephibosheth might have "bartered" to remain hidden?
- When has there been a "knock on the door" in your own life that was unwanted or frightening? (See the examples on pages 69-70.) How does knowing God is with us and wants to help us change the way we respond to these moments?
- Read Matthew 11:28-30 in *THE MESSAGE*. What burdens or weariness do you want to exchange for "the unforced rhythms of grace"? What might it look like to live "freely and lightly"?

Day 5

- Read 2 Samuel 9:5. What thoughts and feelings do you imagine Mephibosheth might have had when he received the king's summons? As you reflect on your own fear of being "found out" or exposed, which of the descriptions on page 75 echo your own experience? What two steps does Lisa suggest for addressing these fears?
- Which of the three scriptures on page 76 most resonate with your heart, and why?

Deeper Conversation *(15 minutes)*

Divide into smaller groups for deeper conversation:

- When have you felt you weren't doing enough—or doing something well enough? What did you believe about yourself in that moment? (page 74)
- Describe how it feels knowing you, too, have a King who asks for your *presence*, not your *perfection*. (page 62)

Closing Prayer *(5 minutes)*

Loving God, You see the wounds we've carried and the labels we've worn, and You call us your chosen and cherished daughters. Replace our cloaks of shame with the robe of Your righteousness. Fix our eyes on your loving gaze and help us to walk in the freedom you make possible for us. We are so grateful that you see us and love us as we are, not as we should be. Help us to hold on to the truth that we are enough because your unfailing love is more than enough. Amen.

WEEK 3

Memory Verse

So let us come boldly to the throne of our gracious God. There we will receive his mercy, and we will find grace to help us when we need it most.

—Hebrews 4:16

The Big Picture

This week we explore how Mephibosheth's tragedy of being dropped and crippled was transformed when he was invited to sit at the king's table for no reason other than his relationship to Jonathan. Likewise, we do nothing to earn redemption but receive it by grace. Here are some key takeaways:

- **Day 1**: Like Mephibosheth before David and Hannah before the Lord, when we bow low in humble surrender and bring our barren, broken places to our King, He meets us there—turning fear into trust, loss into worship, and pain into a sacred place of encounter where we are deeply loved.
- **Day 2**: Though Mephibosheth likely felt small and "not enough" before the king, his story reminds us that when we bring our inadequacy to the One who calls us by name, what we offer becomes enough in His hands—and our worth and dignity are restored.
- **Day 3**: When David told Mephibosheth, "Do not be afraid," it reflected the heart of our faithful King, whose covenant love quiets our fears and invites us to trust Him with a hope-filled future.
- **Day 4:** In 2 Samuel 9:8, when Mephibosheth calls himself "a dead dog," we see how shame can distort our identity; yet his welcome at the king's table reveals that when we step into the light of God's mercy and grace, we are received not as outcasts but as beloved guests.
- **Day 5**: Just as Mephibosheth and Ruth were brought from the margins into a place of honor, God's redeeming grace restores the overlooked and broken, inviting us into His family and His abundant life.

Welcome and Opening Prayer *(5–10 minutes, depending on session length)*
Welcome each woman as she arrives (or joins online) and encourage the women to talk informally until you are ready to open the group in prayer. Use this prayer or offer one of your own:

> *Loving God, as we gather today, we offer You our hearts—which sometimes are broken, weary, or burdened. We acknowledge that we all carry fears, shame, and feelings of inadequacy—and we need You to remind us of our worth in Your eyes. Fill us with courage, hope, and the assurance today that, in Your mercy and grace, we are beloved, restored, and welcomed into Your family. Amen.*

Icebreaker *(5 minutes)*
Invite the women to share short responses to the following question:

- What is one insecurity you had when you were growing up? (They may want to refer to their answers on page 91.)

Video *(20 minutes)*
Play the week 3 video. Invite participants to complete the Video Viewer Guide on page 112 as they watch.

Group Discussion *(25–35 minutes, depending on session length)*

Video

- When has what you had to offer God seemed painfully insufficient? How does the story of the feeding of the five thousand encourage you?
- How have you seen Jesus use "leftovers"—those parts of people's past that they might want to hide or throw away? What part of your imperfect story—the piece you might be tempted to toss aside like a leftover—might Jesus use to comfort or encourage someone else? Who might Jesus be nudging you to comfort and perhaps invite to His table?
- How does John 15:4-5 speak to the truth that on our own we will never be enough, but in Jesus's hands we are more than enough?

Weekly Lessons

Day 1

- How do the stories of Mephibosheth and Hannah echo each other? What do they remind us about our King?
- What are the ways "barrenness" shows up in your life? (page 88)
- According to Hebrews 4:16, how are we to come before God's throne? (page 89) What helps and what hinders you from doing this?

Day 2

- How does David's unconditional welcome of Mephibosheth challenge the way we view God's acceptance of us, especially in moments when we feel inadequate or "not enough"?
- In what ways might embracing the truth that we are held and cherished by God, not because of our perfection but because of His love, change how we approach our fears, relationships, and service?

Day 3

- Read 2 Samuel 9:7a. Why do you think King David told Mephibosheth not to be afraid? Why do you think these words appear so often in Scripture?
- Read aloud Psalm 46:1-2. What are some "mountains of fear" in your life that, with God's help, could crumble? (page 98)
- Read Jeremiah 29:11. How might living with the certainty of this promise change the way you respond to trials, setbacks, or fears? (page 99)

Day 4

- What do Mephibosheth's words in 2 Samuel 9:8 reveal about how he saw himself, and what do they reveal about the fear he likely carried? In what ways does the fear of rejection manifest in your own life—perhaps through striving to be pleasing, perfect, or endlessly available?
- What does Revelation 19:5-8 tells us about our true identity?

Day 5

- In what ways do Ruth and Naomi experience kindness and restoration, and how do you see similar acts of redeeming grace reflected in King David's treatment of Mephibosheth?
- How has God written redemption into a chapter of your life that you thought was over? (page 109)

Deeper Conversation *(15 minutes)*

Divide into smaller groups for deeper conversation:

- In the face of disappointments and tragedy, have you ever wondered if you could trust God? If so, what made trusting God difficult? (page 96)

Closing Prayer *(5 minutes)*

Loving God, You invite us to come boldly before your throne, bringing our disappointments, fears, longings, and questions. Help us to surrender our empty places to you, trusting that you will fill them. We also bring you our hopes—the pieces of ourselves and our lives that seem insufficient—asking you to bless them and multiply what we offer. We desire to trust your timing and your faithfulness more and more. Amen.

WEEK 4

Memory Verse

"Can a mother forget her nursing child?
Can she feel no love for the child she has borne?
But even if that were possible,
I would not forget you!
See, I have written your name on the palms of my hands."
—Isaiah 49:15-16a

The Big Picture

This week we see that like Mephibosheth, who continually sat at the king's table not for provision but for relationship, we are invited by our King to rest in His presence. He asks us to bring not our performance but simply our hearts, our trust, and our desire for His company. Here are a few key takeaways:

- **Day 1**: After years of hiding in fear, Mephibosheth was finally welcomed into a family, a royal family, who embraced him despite his brokenness; similarly, our King invites us into His royal family, desiring not only to provide for us but also to share life with us.
- **Day 2**: Though Mephibosheth may have come to the king's table burdened by labels and loss, the delight in David's gaze likely freed him to rest as a beloved son—just as God's delight in us quiets our shame and reminds us who we truly are.
- **Day 3**: Mica's quiet presence in Scripture reminds us that even after devastating loss, God's covenant mercy endures; His promises ripple through generations, preserving hope in ways we may not immediately see.
- **Day 4**: Seen through Jesus's compassionate eyes, Mary, Martha, and Mephibosheth remind us that God does not ask us to carry life alone but lovingly invites us to lay down our striving and receive His rest.

- **Day 5**: Mephibosheth's disability reminds us that neither our strengths nor our limitations determine our worth. We are welcomed to the King's table as we are; and when we stop measuring ourselves against others, we discover the quiet miracle of being exactly who God designed us to be.

Welcome and Opening Prayer *(5–10 minutes, depending on session length)*
Welcome each woman as she arrives (or joins online) and encourage the women to talk informally until you are ready to open the group in prayer. Use this prayer or offer one of your own:

> *Loving King, thank You for welcoming us into your royal family. As we gather today, remind us that this welcome is not dependent on anything we do but solely on your covenant love. Quiet the labels we carry and the shame we hide, which perpetuate comparison and anxious striving, and help us to rest in Your presence as beloved daughters. Amen.*

Icebreaker *(5 minutes)*
Invite the women to share short responses to the following question:

- What is something you fret about that others barely notice? (They may want to refer to their answers on page 123.)

Video *(20 minutes)*
Play the week 4 video. Invite participants to complete the Video Viewer Guide on page 145 as they watch.

Group Discussion *(25–35 minutes, depending on session length)*
Video

- What are some ways we can be modern-day Marthas, striving so hard that we become worried and upset? In what ways do you find yourself trying to prove your worth—to others or to God?
- What might it look like for us, like Mary, to choose presence over pressure in our daily lives? How might God be inviting you to rest more deeply in His presence?

- Lisa says that Jesus wasn't correcting Martha's activity but was rescuing her heart. How might this compassionate perspective of Jesus change the way you respond to stress and busyness—both your own and that of others? In what areas of your life might Jesus be concerned about rescuing your heart rather than correcting your activity?

Weekly Lessons

Day 1

- How often did Mephibosheth eat at the king's table? How might we make a case that his greater need was not food but the king's presence and a sense of belonging? How might we recognize and prioritize the deeper longings of our own hearts for God's companionship?
- As one accustomed to barley bread being the main course, what do you imagine Sheth might have thought and felt at King David's table? (page 119)
- How does remembering Jesus as the "bread of life" and His sacrifice for us shape the way we approach both our relationship with Him and our connection with others in community?

Day 2

- Read 2 Samuel 9:11b. What does the last phrase tell us about how Mephibosheth was treated? (page 122) How does knowing that, like David with Mephibosheth, God focuses on *who we are* rather than our brokenness change the way we see ourselves and approach Him in relationship?
- Read aloud Zephaniah 3:17. How did you feel after meditating on this verse this week? (page 123) What might it look like for you to allow God to delight in you and sing over you, and how might this change the way you carry your brokenness, worries, and fears in daily life?
- Why do you think we, as women, struggle to delight in ourselves? How might our struggle to delight in ourselves keep us from fully trusting that our unseen King truly takes joy in us?

Day 3

- Read aloud 2 Samuel 9:21a. Why is it so significant that Mephibosheth had a son? What does this reveal to us about our God?
- Discuss the three verses Lisa shared that have helped her to overcome fear: 1 Peter 5:8; Ephesians 6:12; and Deuteronomy 31:6. How do these verses encourage your heart related to your own fears?
- What is the "even if" faith proclamation of Shadrach, Meshach, and Abednego? Have you ever offered an "even if" faith declaration in prayer? If so, how did you sense Jesus walking with you through that fiery trial?

Day 4

- What does Mephibosheth's story teach us about God's provision and the importance of accepting help, and how might this encourage us to lay down our busyness and receive His rest?
- When have you become distracted by the details, like Martha, and found yourself shifting toward a burdened heart? (page 135) Which factors on page 136 tend to most influence your heart attitude while serving?
- What stands out most from your study of Luke 10:38-42 this week?

Day 5

- Read aloud 2 Samuel 9:13. In what ways does Mephibosheth's being crippled in both feet help us rethink how we view our own limitations, and how might that perspective change the way we receive God's love and invitation?
- Have you ever compared yourself to the Proverbs 31 woman—or a spiritual woman you admire? If so, how did that make you feel? (page 142) How do such comparisons affect the way we see ourselves? How can remembering that the Proverbs 31 woman was not a real person but an acrostic portrait from King Lemuel's mother help us let go of comparison and embrace the grace-filled women God has made us to be?

- According to 1 Peter 3:3-4, what matters and what doesn't? What are we to cultivate? (page 143) What helps you to do this?

Deeper Conversation *(15 minutes)*

Divide into smaller groups for deeper conversation:

- What fear might God be inviting you to surrender so its grip no longer holds you captive? (page 131)

Closing Prayer *(5 minutes)*

Jesus, your presence is what sustains and satisfies us. We're tired of striving, comparing, and carrying heavy burdens. We long to sit at your table and bask in the warmth of your approval. Forgive us for getting distracted by the details. Help us to refocus on you and the unique gifts and callings you've given us. We love you, Lord. Amen.

WEEK 5

Memory Verse

I have hidden your word in my heart,
that I might not sin against you.
I praise you, O LORD;
teach me your decrees.
—Psalm 119:11-12

The Big Picture

This week we see that even though Mephibosheth was welcomed to the king's table, he still faced battles and betrayals. We, too, will encounter difficulties, but staying close to our King brings peace and contentment that leads to a truly fulfilled life. Here are some key takeaways:

- **Day 1**: Even amid betrayal, chaos, and the consequences of David's and others' sins—as seen in Mephibosheth's story—we can find refuge and assurance in the One who sees us, fights for us, and secures our victory in love.
- **Day 2**: Mephibosheth's unkept appearance and heartfelt welcome of David shows that God values our devotion and love above appearances, reminding us that we are beloved even in our brokenness and can approach Him with honest hearts.
- **Day 3**: Mephibosheth's unwavering loyalty to David, even in the face of slander and personal risk, reminds us of the importance of loyal friends who mourn with us, celebrate with us, and lift us up in every season.
- **Day 4**: Mephibosheth's humble gratitude, resting fully in David's grace rather than entitlement, reminds us to serve and celebrate from a heart anchored in joy and thankfulness rather than duty or comparison.
- **Day 5**: Mephibosheth's gratitude and contentment—valuing David's presence above his possessions—contrasts with the rich man in Luke 18, reminding us that when we release our attachments and trust the King, we can fully receive His grace and rest at His table.

Welcome and Opening Prayer *(5–10 minutes, depending on session length)*
Welcome each woman as she arrives (or joins online) and encourage the women to talk informally until you are ready to open the group in prayer. Use this prayer or offer one of your own:

> *Loving God, in this broken world we experience brokenness and betrayals, yet we give thanks that our victory is secure in your love. As we gather to learn from your Word, teach us to serve and celebrate others with hearts of gratitude, to be loyal and loving friends, and to let go of the things that keep us from fully surrendering to you. Our desire is to sit at your table and rest in Your presence. May that always be more than enough for us. Amen.*

Icebreaker *(5 minutes)*
Invite the women to share short responses to the following question:

- What is something that helps you to experience peace and contentment?

Video *(20 minutes)*
Play the week 5 video. Invite participants to complete the Video Viewer Guide on page 180 as they watch.

Group Discussion *(25–35 minutes, depending on session length)*
Video

- What qualities of true friendship did Lisa highlight in the video? What other qualities would you add to the description of a true friend?
- Can you think of people who have stood by you like family—and in what ways have you been that kind of faithful friend to others?
- Lisa asked what pieces of the pie we will entrust to God—family, finances, friendships, identity, dreams, and decisions. Are there pieces of the pie that are more challenging for you to entrust fully to God, and if so, why?

Weekly Lessons

Day 1

- In 2 Samuel 13–14 we read about a tragic family conflict that would eventually divide not only David's household but also the kingdom. What events set this conflict in motion, and how did David's failure to address the wrongdoing and pursue reconciliation allow the situation to escalate?
- We learn that Ahithophel was Bathsheba's grandfather. How might David's past actions toward Bathsheba and Uriah have influenced Ahithophel's loyalty years later? How does this remind us that the consequences of our actions can ripple through our families and relationships for years to come? How have you seen this to be true?
- Read aloud 2 Samuel 16:1-4. When Ziba brought provisions to David, whose harvest do you suppose he was actually "gifting" to him? What did David give Ziba in return, and what stands out to you about David's response? (page 153)

Day 2

- What clues in Mephibosheth's appearance and actions in 2 Samuel 19:24 help us understand the condition of his heart while David was gone, and why does that matter in the larger story? How does his response to David's absence remind us of what God values when He looks at us?
- Read 1 Samuel 16:7 aloud. Then share the responses from your own experiences related to what other people notice versus what God notices. (page 159)

Day 3

- After hearing Mephibosheth's explanation in 2 Samuel 19:25-27, what details in the story make you wonder about Ziba's motives and the truth of his earlier report to David? If Ziba did deceive David, what motives do you believe might have driven him—such as resentment, ambition, or envy—and how do those possibilities shape the way you read this part of the story?

- What do the German words *Schadenfreude* and *Freudenfreude* mean, and when have you experienced each?

Day 4

- Read 2 Samuel 19:27-28. How do Mephibosheth's words reveal his attitude of gratitude? (page 177) How does his response contrast with the attitude of the older brother in Luke 15:11-28?
- What helps to cultivate a heart like Mephibosheth's—one that receives love with gratitude and rejoices when others are blessed?

Day 5

- What does the story of the rich man in Luke 18 teach us about unhealthy attachments and contentment?
- Which "tent" are you living under right now—disconTENTment or conTENTment? (page 176) What are you holding that you need to soften your grip on so you may open your hands and your heart to God?
- How does David respond to Mephibosheth in 2 Samuel 19:29, and what do you think might have influenced his decision? What does Mephibosheth's reply in verse 30 reveal about what he values most of all and what makes him content? (page 177)

Deeper Conversation *(15 minutes)*

Divide into smaller groups for deeper conversation:

- Where have you seen disorder or tension in your life that might be caused by jealousy or selfish ambition? How have you responded to that tension, and what has it produced in you or in others? (page 163)

Closing Prayer *(5 minutes)*

Loving God, we are grateful that our victory in this broken world rests securely in your hands. You see every wound and stand as our defender and healer. Grow and mature us so we may rejoice with those who rejoice and weep with those who weep. Anchor us in the confidence that Your love is more than enough—for us and for everyone around us. Teach us to serve You not out of duty, but from delight. May we seek not earthly treasures but the lasting treasure of Your presence. Amen.

WEEK 6

Memory Verse

"I will teach all your children,
and they will enjoy great peace."
—Isaiah 54:13

The Big Picture

This week we explored how Mephibosheth's story reminds us that though we come to the King broken and undeserving, we are welcomed to His table where we are redeemed, restored, and forever secure in the unearned and unfailing love that calls us His beloved children.

- **Day 1**: Like Mephibosheth and the guests in the parable of the king's wedding banquet in Matthew 22, we are called to respond to our King's invitation with faithful presence, gratitude, and trust in His care.
- **Day 2**: Like Mephibosheth at King David's table, we are called by name and invited into God's presence (2 Samuel 9:7; Isaiah 43:1), where our true and unchanging identity as His beloved children is secured and fully known, with a new name whispered to our hearts (Revelation 2:17).
- **Day 3**: Like Mephibosheth at King David's table, we are invited to live in God's kingdom now, embracing our God-given purpose and joyfully extending invitations to others through acts of love, mercy, and goodness while awaiting the fullness of His reign to come.
- **Day 4**: Like Mephibosheth and Dorcas, our ordinary gifts and faithful service, lived for God and others, become an extraordinary, lasting legacy that builds His kingdom and blesses generations (1 Corinthians 12:4-6).
- **Day 5**: Mephibosheth's story shows that even in our brokenness we are deeply loved and chosen. As we receive and embody the King's *hesed* love, we are able to love others the way God loves us, lifting them up and trusting that love is the way God overcomes evil with good in our world.

Welcome and Opening Prayer *(5–10 minutes, depending on session length)*
Welcome each woman as she arrives (or joins online) and encourage the women to talk informally until you are ready to open the group in prayer. Use this prayer or offer one of your own:

> *Loving and gracious King, thank You for calling us by name and inviting us to Your table. As we gather, open our hearts and teach us to how live in your kingdom, using our gifts to serve and love others. Fill us with your* hesed *love so we can lift others up, trusting that Your goodness and love will always triumph. In Jesus's precious name we pray. Amen.*

Icebreaker *(5 minutes)*
Invite the women to share short responses to the following question:

- Picture yourself stepping out to gather manna with the Israelites in the wilderness. Are you laughing with the women beside you, grateful for this daily miracle? Or are you half-awake and quietly grumbling, trying to imagine one more way to prepare the same heavenly provision? (They may want to refer to their answers on page 186.)

Video *(20 minutes)*
Play the week 6 video. Invite participants to complete the Video Viewer Guide on page 213 as they watch.

Group Discussion *(25–35 minutes, depending on session length)*
Video

- Share your thoughts about the "The Love Challenge": Make every ordinary outing a series of mini mission trips—small intentional moments to scatter love, joy, peace, patience, kindness, goodness, gentleness, faithfulness, and self-control wherever you go.
- Who was Barnabas and how did he play a part in shaping Christian history? What was his legacy? How does he show us that encouragement is a force that shapes destinies?
- How might God be calling you to be an encourager like Barnabas?

Weekly Lessons

Day 1

- Deuteronomy 8:2-3 and Mephibosheth's story remind us to rely on God's daily provision and presence. When you come to the King's table, are you showing up with joyful presence like Mephibosheth, or do you treat it more as duty or interruption? What might it look like to honor His invitation with delight rather than obligation?
- How does the parable of the king's wedding banquet in Matthew 22:1-14 show us that our King desires our presence more than our perfection? How would truly believing this affect how you live and respond to His grace?

Day 2

- What does Galatians 4:6 teach us about our deepest identity? How does this perspective change the way you view accomplishments, knowledge, or titles? And how might it shape the way you see yourself, especially if your earthly father fell short?
- Read aloud Isaiah 43:1; 49:15-16a; and Revelation 2:17. How do the details in these verses help you understand your identity and value in God's eyes?

Day 3

- What does 1 Timothy 2:1-4 urge us to do—and why? Share the name of the person you wrote on the invitation on page 198 and your desire for them to experience the joy of salvation.
- Read Matthew 28:19-20. Do you feel called to invite others into discipleship? If so, explain how you are most comfortable extending this invitation. If not, what concerns are holding you back? (page 198)
- When you consider your hope as a believer, what story of how Jesus met you in your deepest need comes to mind? (page 201)

Day 4

- What was the legacy of Dorcas's life? What would you like your legacy to be? How might the gifts and service you already offer, big or small, be used to build God's kingdom and bless others for years to come?
- Read aloud 1 Peter 4:10. Why have we been given spiritual gifts? How does this make you feel? (page 207)

Day 5

- King David lifted Sheth up when he was young, and years later, Sheth encouraged David in his old age—a circle of grace. Who has blessed you in the past, and how might you now be a blessing to them? (page 209)
- How have you experienced God's love, faithfulness, or restoration in your own life during this study? What have you heard God whisper to you these past six weeks that you don't want to forget? (page 211)

Deeper Conversation *(15 minutes)*

Divide into smaller groups for deeper conversation:

- Ask those who have journeyed through this study with you what gifts and talents they have observed in you. Oftentimes, others see our gifts more clearly than we do—and they're more likely to name them.

Closing Prayer *(5 minutes)*

Loving God, though the world gives us many names, none defines us like the one You have spoken over each of us since before time began: Yours. You see our brokenness, yet You call us dearly loved. Thank you for inviting us into Your Kingdom—both now and yet to come—and choosing us to carry Your invitation to others. Help us to see each person as someone You dearly love and long to welcome. Remind us that simply by sharing Your love, we can leave a beautiful legacy that impacts eternity. We love you! Amen.

Group Roster

Name	Phone	Email

Notes

Week 1

1. John H. Walton, *Chronological and Background Charts of the Old Testament* (Zondervan, 1994), 34.

Week 2

1. Trent C. Butler, ed., *Holman Bible Dictionary* (Holman Bible Publishers, 1991), s.v. "Meribbaal."
2. Butler, *Holman Bible Dictionary*, s.v. "Mephibosheth."
3. Butler, *Holman Bible Dictionary*, s.v. "Lo-debar."
4. Butler, *Holman Bible Dictionary,* s.v. "Makirk."

Week 3

1. Chad Brand, Charles Draper, and Archie England, eds., *Illustrated Bible Dictionary* (Holman Bible Publishers, 2003), s.v. "Samuel."
2. John H. Walton and Craig S. Keener, eds., *NIV Cultural Backgrounds Study Bible* (Grand Rapids, MI: Zondervan, 2016), note on John 6:9.
3. Attributed to Zig Ziglar.

Week 4

1. Shmuel and Ze'ev Safrai, *The Jewish People in the First Century,* vol. 2 (Fortress Press, 1976), 770–771, noting the postexilic introduction of domestic fowl into Judean agriculture.
2. Brand et al., *Holman Illustrated Bible Dictionary*, s.v. "Micah."
3. American Psychological Association, *Stress in America 2023: A Nation Recovering but Still Under Strain* (American Psychological Association, 2023).
4. For discussion of the Hebrew terms *tov* and *me'od* as they appear in Genesis 1:31, see Ludwig Koehler and Walter Baumgartner, *The Hebrew and Aramaic Lexicon of the Old Testament*, ed. Walter Baumgartner and Johann Jakob Stamm (Brill, 1994); and Francis Brown, S. R. Driver, and Charles A. Briggs, *A Hebrew and English Lexicon of the Old Testament* (Clarendon Press, 1907).
5. Madeleine S. Miller and J. Lane Miller, *Harper's Bible Dictionary* (Harper & Row, 1981), 441.
6. Jessica Koehler, "Cultivating a Gratitude Habit for Improved Well-Being: A Grateful Mind," *Psychology Today*, updated November 23, 2023, https://www.psychologytoday.com/us/blog/beyond-school-walls/202304/cultivating-a-gratitude-habit-for-improved-well-being.

7. Kori D. Miller, "14 Benefits of Practicing Gratitude," PositivePsychology.com, June 18, 2019, https://positivepsychology.com/benefits-of-gratitude/.

Week 6

1. Compare the Hebrew form *Elisheva',* meaning "my God is an oath."
2. The term used is *mathētria*, the feminine form of *mathētēs* ("disciple"). This is the only occurrence of the feminine noun for "disciple" in the New Testament, making Tabitha/Dorcas the only individual in Scripture explicitly identified with this title.